Learning in Relationship

Foundation for Personal and Professional Success

by Ronald R. Short, Ph.D.

To purchase additional copies of this book or to obtain information about additional here–and–now learning resources, contact *Learning in Action Technologies, Inc.*, 12819 SE 38th Street, PMB 264, Bellevue, Washington 98006-1395. (425) 641-7246. Fax (425) 401-6998.

www.learninginaction.com

Printed in the United States of America

First Edition

ISBN #1–887259–01–5

Cover Illustration by Abby Levine
Book Layout and Design by Symmetria

Contents

Dedication

This book is dedicated to two psychologists who shaped my reality as a young graduate student because they challenged mainstream psychological theory.

While immersed in the implications of reductionism, logical positivism, laboratory experimentation and strict empiricism, my experience was validated by *Carl Rogers* and his "primacy of the subjective."

While studying models of learning, development and personality, all assuming causation from the past, my world was expanded and challenged by *Kurt Lewin* and his "principle of contemporaneity."

Acknowledgements

My greatest thanks is to the hundreds of students whom I knew in the Masters program at the Leadership Institute of Seattle (LIOS). Their struggles toward personal integrity in relationship provided the opening into the hidden realities that are made explicit in this book.

The support, dialogue and freedom to experiment with colleagues was essential. Thank you Bob Crosby, John Scherer, Barbara Arney, Brenda Kerr, Denny Minno, Judy Heinrich, John Runyan, David Erb and Rhonda Gordon.

I was impressed by the willingness of colleagues to read drafts and give me feedback. Thanks Geoff Bellman, Bill Brasswell, David Bradford, Glenn Bucholtz, Gervase Busche, Gary Crowell, Dell Drake, Ruth Emory, Molly Gibbs, Jim Helwig, Gary Jusela, Kris King, Michael Marlowe, Art McNeil, Barbara McMahon, Rene Pino, Leo Seguel, Peter Senge, Rick Redmond, Rick Ross, Charlie Seashore, Christine Sanchez, Sharon Thorne, Pat Walker, Wayne Wanner, Richard Webster, and Bob Woodruff. The book would not be as clear without you.

Mary Ann Owen, you were a great editoral help as you knew what I wanted to say and helped me say it better. I am indebted to you, D.J. Raines, for the extraordinary effort, energy, thought and creativity you put into formatting and design. I consider myself lucky to have found the two of you.

Finally, thank you Janet Johnson. You gave me space, accepted my crazy fits of anxiety, listened to help me get clear, edited my writing, and loved me through it all.

This Book is For. . .

Organizational practitioners who, regardless of role, need to navigate in the "permanent white water*" of organizational change, who recognize they cannot do it alone, and who want to integrate learning with doing;

Teams that want to be their best, avoid and correct group stupidities, and are willing to learn, apply and monitor the disciplined skills necessary;

Partners of all kinds who want to make their relationships work; and

Individuals who value their personal integrity and want to express it in their work and personal relationships.

To help address these human challenges, the book will invite you to:

- name what you already sense;
- recognize what has always been in front of you;
- grasp the significance of naming what has been there all along; and
- use these newly named truths for a lifetime of learning.

* Image from Peter Vaill, 1996.

Read This Introduction
(*Even if you don't read introductions*)

Stripped to its essence, this book is about how to learn from others who have different perspectives. Let's begin now, between you and me.

You are probably reading this for the first time, perhaps to decide whether you want to read further.

I am writing this introduction after months of struggle, fearful that the book may not come together. I have begun this book several times; gone to sleep at night and awakened in the morning thinking about it; carried a cassette recorder with me to capture fleeting ideas; postponed other professional goals; put my life on hold until the book was written.

You can see that we approach the book from very different perspectives. While you are freely deciding whether to read it, I am its prisoner.

My struggle has had value, however. I now know more about myself and understand what my emotional commitment is all about. It's not true that I've been writing this book for a few months—I have been working on it all my personal and professional life.

My passion for these ideas started early. As a boy my job in the family was to bring peace at those inevitable times of tension. During those times words often carried an opposite meaning. "Don't worry about me" meant that somebody better worry! I learned to listen and interpret what the words *really* meant.

At 64, I can now see that those early experiences organized my entire professional career as an educator, psychologist

This book is about how to learn from others who have different perspectives.

1

and consultant toward a singular purpose—*To help people learn to talk straight so they can learn from each other.*

Those professional years have given me a window into a reality that I simply have to share. I have been witness to thousands of difficult interactions that, if tweaked only slightly, could have produced massive savings in pain and wasted resources. I have noticed again and again the transformation that takes place in organizations and teams when people truly understand and implement this fundamental message:

Communicating isn't about doing it right the first time. It's about learning from each other—especially when communications go wrong.

I now know with certainty that:

- A huge amount of the human pain and wasted resources that takes place in organizations is preventable and certainly correctable.

- These costs are seldom because of malevolent intent or difficult individuals, but because of interactions that produce missing, misattributed, misinterpreted information.*

- Other individuals or groups, *not* the interactions and relationships, get the blame. This very predictable human reflex blocks information and prevents learning.

- Our understanding of how and why all the above works is greatly oversimplified.

In short, we muck around in this mess together and have inadequate maps to get us out.

Notice that I use "us" and "we," the plural, the collective. The above statements pertain to all of us. We are caught in

> *A huge amount of the human pain and waste of resources that takes place in organizations is preventable.*

---

* To seem credible, I must say that I realize there are individuals who cannot learn and who are difficult or impossible to deal with. However, I write this book to the majority of healthy, well–intentioned, competent people who want to make a constructive contribution. As we learn to learn from each other, the power of those other rare individuals will be minimized.

this together. However, I haven't written this book to the crowd, the organization, the team, or even to partners. I've written it "to one individual at a time" (to paraphrase the advertisement). I've written it to *you*.

Why? Because while we all participate in this collective issue, there are no corporate initiatives, no razzle–dazzle training, selling, telling, explaining, coercing or flattering that can make you learn anything from anybody else. You simply have to make that choice for yourself.

The responsibility is yours and yours alone. The freedom is yours. The consequences are yours, and you'll find that, like me, you face this choice several times a day, in many different contexts, with just about everybody. This book is designed to help you make those choices.

Where will you find the information to make these choices? It is not where you might expect—on the internet, in the media, in some book or library, or in some outside expert. Rather, it lies hidden within, among and between you and those from whom you need to learn. The information you need is always present, all the time, always here and now.

This means you have to become your expert. I have to become mine. At the heart of our expertise is awareness.

So, this is a different kind of book. It is not about skills and techniques to use on others as separate objects. It is a guide to help increase your awareness—increase your choice—and increase your freedom with all the personal integrity, responsibility and accountability those ideas imply.

About the Book

Part 1 of this book, **Thinking Lessons**, introduces you to an interpersonal world that is in front of you, around you, and among you. You'll be given "lenses," ways of thinking, that open you to this ever–present world.

Armed with this perspective, **Part 2, Inquiry Lessons** provides core principles and assumptions that prepare you to learn from your relationships in the present tense—from what is going on here and now:

- *among* you and others;
- *between* you and one other person; and
- *within* you.

In **Part 3, Application Lessons**, you'll learn how to put the new perspectives to work in "real time" with "real people" while "real issues" are going on. The lessons provide step–by–step methods you can use to learn from each perspective. The lessons end with three practice exercises that you can use on your own.

This is not a scholarly book and, therefore, I make very few bibliographic references in the text. However, it would be a great mistake to ignore the fact that while this book represents my synthesis, every single idea stands on the shoulders of so many other theoreticians, practitioners and researchers. I mention a very few in **References, Influences and Resources**.

Part 1
Thinking Lessons

The critical path to learning relationships begins with the ability to think differently.

Thinking Lessons

You are not alone if you are turned off by the word *learning*. Your eyes may glaze over with images of classrooms, stand–and–deliver training, textbooks, lectures, tests and grades. Learning from other individuals is very different. You won't learn *about* communications or be tested on it. You won't learn about principles of *how to* communicate. Rather, you will learn *how well* you are communicating, and *what* you are communicating to the particular person(s) in front of you.

This is how it works.

Learning Relationships and Learning Cultures

You share a basic dilemma with everybody else on the planet. You live a rich life inside your head. You continually react, interpret, infer, and provide meaning to what happens to you. You create, author, edit, produce, direct and act in your own internal drama. Others can't know what goes on inside you unless you tell them, but they often *assume* they do—so they don't ask.

Others have rich lives inside their heads as well. They also react, interpret, infer, and provide meaning to what happens to them. You can't know what it is unless they tell you, but you often *assume* you do—so you don't inquire.

Everything flows from these simple facts.
As you go through life doing whatever you do, other folks make *their* sense out of *your* actions. You do the same to them. You create stories about them—why they do what they do; what they

are like; and what they must want, feel and think. Your stories are real to you, and they may be accurate—but then again, they may not. Others' stories are real to them; likewise, they may be accurate—then again, they may not.

Because you cannot know what is in another person's head unless you are told, you are confronted with the fundamental, existential, social predicament that happens simply because you are human—you are often not aware that you are not aware. *You don't know what you don't know—and you don't know that you don't know.*

The problem is that we don't know what we don't know.

The only way out of this dilemma is to learn from each other in the moment. The only way you can learn is for both you and others to describe your stories about each other and inquire whether they are accurate. Since you are the authors of your stories, learning from each other means to compare stories and then edit or even rewrite them based upon the new information.

At the simplest level, learning from others means that you do four things:

1. acknowledge that what is in your head is a story that *you* are making up;
2. share it;
3. inquire about the other person's story; and
4. revise your story based upon the new information.

You can see that this is not about the classroom, being trained, zoning out in a lecture, or taking tests. It's not about being bored. It is far more about being scared. It's about being real, taking risks, and trusting yourself to be who you are.

This is pretty risky, so you may do what folks normally do—sit around and wait for others to make it safe before you share your story. While you do that, you can write elaborate stories about why it is unsafe for you to speak out, why others are not sharing theirs, and what is wrong with all these folks anyway. You can live a rich internal life.

The problem, of course, is that others do the same thing––wait for you and others to make it safe for them. When everybody waits on everybody else, everybody lives with their internal story, for the most part assuming that they are accurate.

The answer to this human dilemma is not easy because we need to risk before we can trust—not the other way around.

To illustrate what I mean, imagine for a moment that you just arrived at a four–day training with 23 others. You know a few of the other participants superficially but are meeting the others for the first time. The word about this seminar ranges from good to ecstatic, but you've also heard a couple of others say it was a waste of time.

Regardless, everybody agreed that the learning was intense. Therefore, you arrive expecting something other than the basic stand–and–deliver, watch–the–video, take–notes and role–play type of training. You know that you will be invited to be the real you, not play a simulated role or person.

You walk in the door somewhat anxious and notice the same is true for others. People are eating, drinking cup after cup of coffee, shuffling their feet, laughing nervously. The four folks who must be the staff are conversing up front by the typical flip charts. You are not made more comfortable by noticing the videotape camera at the side of the room.

After everyone gets acquainted, the stage is set for the training and you go into action. You are partnered with another participant who will coach you. The two of you set your goals, then agree on how you can be helpful to each other.

Your group is then given a task:

> "The six of you will be together as a group for the entire week. Your goal is to become a high performance learning team. Your task for the next 30 minutes is to agree

We need to risk before we can trust—not the other way around.

upon how the group must function in order to achieve this goal. Write five to seven guidelines on newsprint."

My colleagues and I have given this task to literally hundreds of groups over the years as a way to build teams. Our purpose was to get them into action, begin the process of learning, and apply the skills that we provided throughout the remainder of the week.

It took me a very long time to notice what was under my nose time and time again. Every group proceeded to accomplish the task in a variety of ways, but they *all*, independently and without coaching, discussed and wrote the *same* aspirations. With semantic variations, it was inevitable that words and guidelines such as "open," "honest," "trust," "risk," "listening," "respect" and "straight feedback" were represented on *every single one* of the hundreds of sheets.

We *never* had a team say they wanted to be fearful, to mistrust or be closed with each other. However, you wouldn't know it by their actions. On a regular basis they were tentative; they hid, ducked, dodged, weaved and obfuscated; they gossiped; at times they were even accusatory and blamed the staff for their discomfort. What they wanted and how they behaved were 180 degrees apart.

It is truly ironic how adeptly they shot themselves in the foot by waiting to trust before they risked. Mistrust became the norm.

However (and this is the critical point), when the individuals in the group finally got fed up with what was happening and shared their internal stories ("I am anxious," or "I am totally confused") they were able to achieve the mutual trust and respect they wanted in the first place.

Collectively they created their learning culture, and it always started by one person simply deciding to tell his or her truth.

When we do not take risks and share our stories, we take a much greater risk—that fear and mistrust will rule.

We all face this dilemma. When we do not take risks and share our stories, what we truly risk is that fear and mistrust will rule. We refuse to communicate directly, go behind people's backs, and only talk to those who share our views. We ignore advice, embarass and blame others, and avoid bringing up obvious problems. We distort our communications. As a result, we can easily find ourselves immersed in a toxic pool of poor morale, bad decisions, pain and waste—all of our own making.

As an example of the toxic results of mistrust, I recently talked to a manager for a company with multiple production sites. In a moment of candor he said, "I am embarrassed to say this, and of course I don't do it publicly, but before the managers became a team, I actually used to celebrate when another site reported an accident. It made me and my shop look good. I think all of the site managers thought this way."

Unfortunately, it is all too easy for us to live *down* to others' expectations.

Fear and mistrust are as contagious as a Topanga Canyon fire in hot Santa Ana winds. I doubt seriously whether any other human condition is so self–fulfilling, self–perpetuating and costly as mistrust. When it comes to mistrust, what goes around truly comes around. Mistrust others and they will mistrust you (and give you good reason to mistrust them while you're giving them good reasons to mistrust you).

Learning equips you to be an antidote to this kind of toxicity. Trust and mutual respect are highly desired and also very contagious. I base my professional life upon the fact that when people know how to create trust, mutual respect and a learning culture, for the most part, they will do so.

Succinctly, a *learning culture is a collective state where people are expected to share information that lies inside,* where you and your colleagues edit and rewrite your stories about each other. By doing this, you truly live up to your aspirations, rather than down to your fears. *In a learning culture, there is minimal discrepancy between what you collectively want and how you behave.*

However, because we have to risk to develop trust, a learning culture cannot be mandated, ordered or commanded. It has to grow from the inside–out by individual choice. It starts with you. It starts with me.

Learning How to Learn Starts with Thinking

Why thinking lessons? Because how we collectively think *is* the problem. It blinds us to information. Quite simply, we cannot get out of our messes if we continue to think the thoughts that put us there in the first place.

A learning culture is a collective state where you and your colleagues edit and rewrite your stories about each other.

Have you ever rifled through a junk drawer to find something when someone reached over your shoulder, picked up the object and handed it to you? It was there all along, right under your nose. Somewhat embarrassing, isn't it? Especially if you just muttered something like "Who took the (expletive deleted) tape?!"

Psychologists call this phenomenon a "perceptual set." It is an expectation of how the item looks, its position, condition, color, or shape. It's difficult to find if it doesn't conform to our perceptual set. We essentially create an image of the way something is supposed to look in our heads. When reality doesn't match our image, we simply do not see it. We all understand this at the personal level.

Now, what if you and your colleagues all had the same perceptual set? Broader than that, what if we all have the same perceptual sets? And, what if they are *not* in alignment with the truth? Then nobody sees the obvious. We would not see what was right in front of us. What's more, there would be nobody to

12

reach over our shoulders to point out the obvious. We would be blind to the the reality in front of us. I think this is the case.

As a young faculty member on a small college campus years ago, a botanist faculty colleague led me around to learn the local northwest flora and fauna. Before the tour, it is fair to say that I was somewhat limited in my ability to name, recognize and differentiate among the campus vegetation; that is, I was at the grass–bush–tree level.

When we ended our tour, I was amazed at the incredibly diverse array of vegetation that I had walked around and tromped on for years. I learned something about vegetation, and a lot about what I did not know. However, the most powerful lesson for me was that without the concepts, the different forms of vegetation *did not exist for me*. With the new concepts, I was able to see what had been there all along.

Over the years I have taken similar tours through relationships. I learned concepts that enable me to see what I was blind to before.

Therefore, think of the thinking lessons as a guided tour through your interactions and relationships. I'll give you ways to think and concepts that enable you to see what is (and has always been) in front of you. Like the campus vegetation, so much of the information you need in order to learn from other people is not distant, disconnected, esoteric, and obscure. Rather, it is right here, right now; it is in front, inside and around you—waiting to be named.

We create an image of the way something is supposed to look; when reality doesn't match our image, we simply do not see it.

13

Short Takes

■ You constantly write stories about yourself and others inside your head.

■ If you choose to learn, you must risk, share your stories and revise them.

■ You create learning relationships when you mutually share your stories and revise them with new information,

■ Learning relationships counter the natural toxicity of mistrust.

■ The critical path to learning relationships begins with thinking differently.

Thinking Lesson 1
IN THE MIDDLE, LOOKING OUT

When you think of groups and organizations doing their thing separate from you, you have to wait on others. You lose choice.

This lesson puts you at the center of *your* relationships, *your* group and *your* organization. When you choose to learn, *your* organization learns. When you choose not to learn, *your* organization does not learn.

This is about empowerment.

Relationships are the very heart and soul of an organization's ability to get any job done.

What images come to mind when you think of the word "organization?" This quotation may shape your understanding of the word.

Relationships are both the building blocks and probably the most telling indicators of the new (participative) governance. In fact, the genetic code of the organization is embedded in thousands of interactions that occur every day between people everywhere in the organization. (McLagan & Nel, 1995.)

Note that this statement makes relationships and interactions more important than whether or not people like to work with each other. Relationships and interactions are not simply components of organizational life that make people happy or sad, or increase or decrease job satisfaction and productivity. They are not just a nice side–effect of being on a team. They are not one of many peripheral elements in getting the job done.

Relationships are the very heart and soul of an organization's ability to get any job done. Whether good or bad, effective or ineffective, relationships and their interactions are the organization's DNA—they create and define organizations. Without them there is no organization.

The essence of an Organization is Relationships

What goes on between individuals defines what an organization is and what it can become.

Nobody can lead unless she or he has a follower *and* a relationship. Nobody can be a customer without a supplier *and* a relationship. That is why relationships and interactions are the "genetic code" of organizations. What goes on *between individuals* defines what an organization is and what it can become.

Think about the reality this idea introduces—you are no longer just an individual, but an individual standing in the middle of many relationship systems. The systems are you, the others and your relationships. Much of what you once thought of as independent actions are now transactions. You are now positioned to notice, not just yourself and other individuals, but the dance that happens between and among you.

Change your part of the dance and you change your organization. Nothing in general happens until something specific happens. Your relationships won't change until you and each of the individuals whom you face daily change how you relate and interact.

This is where your understanding of the word "organi-zation" can get in the way. If you're like most folks, the word "organization" conjures up images and assumptions about an entity that exists "out there" in time and space, probably owned by someone else—a legal abstraction that exists somewhere distant from you. For legal purposes it does.

However, *your* organization is made up of *your* relationships and the very specific interactions *you* have with specific individuals, in specific contexts, over specific issues. You and those with whom you interact define what *your* organization is— and the limits of what *you* can do and become. These interactions are the "genetic code" for *your* organization, and they contain the information you need to learn.

From this inside–out perspective, your organization is no longer NASA, Texaco Oil, IBM, U.S. Army, or the Presbyterian Church. Whether you are a shipping clerk, supervisor, manager, director or president, you define your organization. Think of yourself as smack dab in the center—because you are.

Without you, your organization doesn't exist. Any effort to change your organization has to begin with you and your specific interactions with specific individuals. Why is this realization so important? Because I have seen the opposite assumption play out time and time again. It is far more typical for individuals in an organization or a team to want others to change before they do.

As illustrated earlier, the unstated message in almost every group that I have observed is "everybody else needs to make it safe for me to take a risk," or "everyone else (the boss, the company) has to make everything okay for me before they can expect me to fully participate."

When that is true, there is no change, awareness or learning because everybody waits on everybody else to do it first. Desired changes do not occur, creativity is suppressed, the organization suffers and you suffer.

So, like Kansas, you're in the middle.

Any effort to change your organization must begin with you and your specific interactions with specific individuals.

Why is it we don't see our organizations this way? Why do we overlook information from our relationships? Why don't we recognize our responsibility to learn from them? Why are we predisposed to wait on others?

The next lesson will throw some light on these questions. It is the most important lesson to learn—all the other thinking lessons flow from it.

Short Takes

- Your organization is not an abstraction that floats around out there in space separate from you.
- Your relationships do not exist separate from you and cannot exist or change without you.

Exercise

1. On a blank sheet of paper, define *your* organization by listing the names of the people with whom you work most closely.

2. Choose one relationship that you want to improve or examine and circle the other person's name. (You'll be asked to refer to your relationship with this particular person in the exercises at the end of each Thinking Lesson.)

3. Check your understanding.

   If you are aware that changing this one relationship will change *your* organization, you understand the first lesson.

   If you now realize that when *you* choose not to learn, *your* organization will not learn, you're ready to move on. Congratulations!

Thinking Lesson 2
IN THE MIDDLE, LOOKING INSIDE–OUT

This lesson brings information about *your* relationships, group and organization even closer. You'll discover that they do not exist *out there*, outside of you. They are *in here*, inside of you.

In here is your home—always here, always now, always available. This is where you go to find information, awareness and choice.

This lesson puts you in charge.

The prior lesson was just a warm up. Here comes the tough part, a conceptual shift that is counter intuitive to much of what comes naturally. To all of us, this shift is essential for learning from others. Take your time and let the ideas soak in. They are core to everything that follows.

The key element of Lesson 1 is that *you are in the center of your relationships.* Your relationships do not exist separate from you and cannot exist or change without you. Relationship problems do not start independent of you, and they cannot be resolved independent of you. Relationship (A <–> B) cannot exist without (A) or (B).

Of course, these are obvious statements. When you are in a relationship, it cannot exist without you. Why does it need to be said? Because if you are like most of us, you operate in the world as if you were an observer. The key concept in this lesson is understanding and experiencing *how you see the world and others as outside of and separate from you when they are not.*

A recent experience of mine illustrates this. Not long ago I shared an elevator with two workmen. The elevator stopped on the fifth floor. One man stepped out without checking the floor number and his partner said, "Wrong floor. We're going to the ninth." Here is the important point that says it all—the first man came back into the elevator, glanced at the rest of us, and muttered, "Elevator from hell!"

He located the problem. It was outside of him. The problem was the elevator, not his error.

None of us fellow passengers acknowledged his comment. Bemused, but looking straight ahead as I always do in elevators, I had some fun imagining how I might acknowledge him.

"Yeh. Ain't it the pits? They should do something about it." (Nah, that didn't seem right.)

"I ride it every day and I manage to get off on the right floor most of the time. At least it's never tricked me." (No. That would be sarcastic and he was bigger than me.)

"Well, I disagree. I really like these elevators." (No. Wouldn't go anywhere.)

Frankly I was stuck. Why? Because his comment came from embarrassment, which was *inside* him; and the elevator, which was *outside* of him, was irrelevant.

But lest you think I made fun of him, I was doing the same. I focused outside, on him, when something was going on inside me that motivated me to play with responses. On the inside, I was slightly embarrassed for him, but I was also delighted and amused. He had just given me a simple example I could use in this book.

Judging that the world is outside, distinct and separate from us, is a simple human reflex. We're wired that way.

Both of us had a rich amount of activity going on inside, but we placed it outside on an object and the other.

Him: "That damned elevator!"

Me: "He is embarrassed—too embarrassed to admit it."

None of us is immune. When was the last time you were bugged by someone or something outside, like what someone did or did not do at work? Or you talked critically to a spouse or friend about someone else? Maybe you couldn't sleep because of something that someone did, or you muttered to yourself about someone else. Perhaps you and others on your team groused about what "they" did to you, or prohibited you from doing?

Be honest with yourself now. Do you ask yourself how *you* contribute to the situation when you participate in the above murmuring and muttering? You may eventually catch yourself and wind up thinking you caused the whole problem; but reflexively you initially react because of what someone else *outside* is doing.

The next step is automatic. Since the problem is *outside*, "he," "she," "they" (or the elevator) obviously needs to change. We either live with the problem or try to change it, him, them or her.

This focus outside, on others, becomes *the problem*. There isn't anything as stable and predictable as an organization of all fixers on the hunt for fixees.

This is the way it works, from the most visible to the least visible:

There isn't anything as stable and predictable as an organization full of fixers on the hunt for fixees.

21

We start with what looks like a
work problem

Then it becomes a
problem with another person

As we look deeper, we find it is a
problem with the relationship

Looking deeper, we find that the
problem is trying to fix the other person

At our very core
we find that
the problem is that we think the world is outside of us.

Our biggest, yet least visible, problem is that we think the world is outside of us.

At the foundation, we all have a reflex to focus outside, on the object, on the other. To assume that the world is outside, distinct and separate from us, is a reflex that is simply part of being human. We're wired that way.

Reflexively, we all step off the "elevator from hell." That is our biggest, yet least visible, problem.

Therefore, it is important to realize that you generally cannot learn from others by simply following your reflexes. The perspective you need in order to learn is just the opposite of the way you're wired. Instead of automatically focusing on what you think is *outside*, turn around and focus on what you feel, think and want—*from the inside*. Then bring that into your relationships to learn. Here is an example of questioning from the inside rather than the outside:

Outside	Inside
"Why is she doing that?"	"I'm curious—wonder why I am?"
"She wants to run the place."	"I'm jealous. Do *I* want to run the place?"
"She loves to control."	"I'm bugged! Where does that judgment come from?"
"I wish he'd be happy."	"I'm bored. Why is it so important to me that *he* change?"

Instead of automatically focusing on the outside, turn around and focus inside.

Finally, rather than fix the elevator, turn 180 degrees and simply acknowledge that you're embarrassed.

Think of yourself as a Janus mask with two faces back to back. One faces Inside you, the other faces Outside. Together they create a whole.

Inside ← — —  — — → Outside

These two perspectives are always available to us, in every moment of our conscious lives. To understand what I mean, I'll provide an example using my current reality (March 17, 1998).

When I face only *outside*, I mistakenly ignore what is *inside*. The outside becomes my focus, my "figure," the "cause" of whatever happens inside me. My internal activities become "background." Often I am not conscious of them. This is certainly the dominant experience for most of us, in most situations, most of the time.

Now, I'll turn around, look the other way and face inside. The outside is now "background," and what I think, feel and want inside are the "figure" or "cause" of my response to what is outside. To the elevator man it meant recognizing his embarassment instead of blaming the elevator. This is often difficult to do with undefended honesty. When we face inside, however, we have a very different experience.

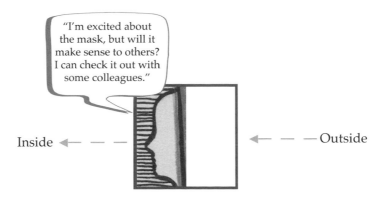

To meet the world from the inside–out means to turn *inside*, identify what is there and then choose whether to bring it back *outside* to the other.

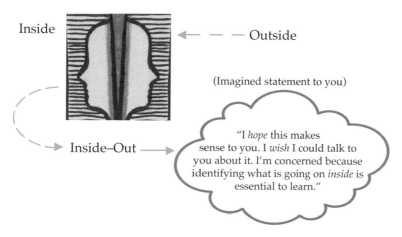

Inside

Outside

(Imagined statement to you)

Inside–Out

"I *hope* this makes sense to you. I *wish* I could talk to you about it. I'm concerned because identifying what is going on *inside* is essential to learn."

To operate from the inside–out means to observe the internal states that drive your response to the outside.

To operate from the inside–out means to observe and describe the motives, intentions, feelings, judgments, and attributions that drive your responses to the other. It is to be in touch with your internal experience.

Until you make this shift, your assumptions, perceptions, and perceptual sets about relationships are not only a little misleading, they are 180 degrees out of whack. You'll look outside for answers when they lie inside. You'll try to change others when you need to change. Not only will you be unable to learn, your efforts will be wasted and often destructive to your relationships.

It is amazingly difficult to make this shift consistently. Once again, it's simply our programming. Our outside orientation is so strong—almost hard wired—that it tricks us time and time again. We think we're being honest with ourselves and others, only to learn that we're not.

We human beings can be very, very tricky this way. That is precisely why it is important to approach this new direction with grace, both for yourself and for others.

Short Takes

■ You are in the center of all your relationships, looking out at others.

■ To learn from your relationships, you must face *inside*, not just *outside*.

■ This is much easier said than done.

Exercise

1. Identify a behavior of the other person you selected earlier that impacts you strongly.

2. Focus only on what is *inside* you *now* as you bring the other person to mind. On a blank sheet of paper, write an attribution. Why do you think the other person behaves that way?

   Write how you feel. (Some derivative of mad, sad, glad or scared.)Write what you want. (*Note: Do not write what you don't want, but what you do want.*)

   Your ability to describe these internal activities is critical to learn from this relationship.

3. Check your understanding. If you can talk about this lesson and then turn inside and describe this lesson's impact on you (what you feel, think and want) while reading it, congratulations! You're on track.

Thinking Lesson 3
LIVING FROM THE INSIDE–OUT

> **You now see that you are *inside* your relationships looking out and they are *inside* you. This lesson emphasizes the idea that at the most basic level, learning from the *inside–out* requires the courage to be yourself.**
>
> **This lesson builds confidence.**

Learning from the inside–out places you on a path that will inevitably lead you into an expanded reality. The longer you practice learning from others, the more you'll find yourself transformed from being a victim–spectator into the slowly dawning awareness that you are a creator–participant. After all, it is one thing to react to what somebody outside is doing *to* you. It is quite another to grow in the realization that what *you* think and how you feel inside shapes your perception and response to what the other is doing.

Let's look at a few implications of this fact.

Your Reality is Fact to You

When you turn your gaze 180 degrees and look inside, what you see, notice and name is real. To illustrate what I mean, let's shift to another image.

When a boy drives a car in an arcade, he has an experience in what is called "virtual reality." This phrase is intended to communicate that the experience *feels* like reality, but is *not* reality. When he accelerates, brakes, turns and spins out, it is a simulation. It is not real, but is a close approximation of what it is like to drive.

Learning to drive, fly or be an astronaut with simulations that create "virtual reality" are extremely useful experiences, as well as entertaining. Since the reality is "virtual," it is far better to spin out or crash in simulation rather than to actually crash and burn.

We call this "virtual" reality because we compare it to the "real" unsimulated world outside ourselves where there are real consequences like crash and burn. Ask any boy whether the arcade experience is real, and he'll give you a funny look. It's a question so dumb he won't even respond. Of course the arcade experience isn't real. Of course there's no real fire, blood and mayhem. Duh!

However, from the inside–out, the fear and excitement are real—they are his actual internal experience (and the whole purpose of creating the simulation!). The mayhem which generates them is not real.

When you turn from viewing others outside and look inside instead, what you see is real. Sure, it may be inaccurate. It is part of the "virtual reality" stories that you create. But what you feel, think and want in this particular relationship, at this particular time, is real. Perhaps you "shouldn't" feel, think or want what you do—but that is irrelevant. Your experience is real to you, and your feelings, thoughts and wants are neither right nor wrong—they just are.

So, just as with the simulations, your outside "reality" may be "virtual," but what is inside of you is real. From the perspective of inside–out, what you think, feel and want is simply not arguable.

Your experience is real to you and your feelings, thoughts and wants are neither right nor wrong—they just are.

You Experience Only Your Reality

When I was a child, I remember staring intently at my brother wondering, "When I see red, does Larry see the same thing? How would I know? Could I ever know?" It occured to me that if I were able to look out through his eyes, I might call it brown. It is very possible that what he calls red and what I see as red are very different colors. . . Larry and I, and everybody else, have simply agreed to call this color red.

Now I understand that we can measure the involvement of the retina, the cones, the frequency of the spectrum, the neural response, and the response in the brain. We know with a high degree of certitude that Larry and I see the same color in the same way.

However, my point is there is no way from the outside–in that I can ever know what it is like from Larry's inside–out. To achieve this, I would have to enter his head, turn around 180 degrees and look out through his eyes. I can only know what it is like for me from the inside–out.

My brother is stuck with his reality and I'm stuck with mine. Our realities inevitably differ, but both are real.

Others Never Experience Your Reality

You have a unique perspective. Just as I can't see Larry's red, he can't see mine. Nobody can see the world the way you do. Nobody can view another person exactly as you do. You are in a totally unique, nonreproducible, nonreplicable, existentially singular position.

The only person who can know what it is like from your perspective is you. You stand alone on your one square foot of earth—nobody else can. The implication of this can be as profound as standing up for your deepest values; or it can be as

Respecting and claiming your perspective while simultaneously being open to others is the key to learning.

29

simple as having the courage to say you're cold when everybody else appears comfortable.

From the outside–in, you and a colleague have one relationship. From the inside–out, there are two—your relationship with him and his relationship with you. From the outside–in, five people can make one team. From the inside–out there are five teams and 20 relationships. From the inside–out, no two children were ever raised in the same family.

To respect and claim your perspective while simultaneously being open to other perspectives is the key to learning.

I believe that is the mature learner's challenge in a nut shell; one that constantly pops up in our faces over and over again. It never goes away. To stand alone on your "square foot of earth" takes the courage to be yourself. *To be open to influence from other perspectives, you risk the discovery that the only reality you have is inaccurate.*

> *To be open to influence from other perspectives, you risk the discovery that the only reality you have is inaccurate.*

Much of What You Think is Outside is, in Fact, Information About You

This is not solipsism or a philosophical exercise. The outside does exist. This is very practical and lies at the heart of learning. Of course others exist separate from you, but *not* when you turn and look inside.

As I discussed in the last lesson, everybody in your conscious life lives his or her life inside of you. Each individual fits into active stories you create about them, your relationship, and yourself. This awareness is critically important to learning from others. *The fundamental implication is that learning from others has little to do with them, and a whole bunch to do with you.*

Therefore, you can direct your energies away from managing others to managing yourself *with* others—from figuring others out to understanding yourself. You can shift your attention from the other to what *you bring to* the other. You can quit wasting time being obsessed with the elevator and take a look at your embarrassment.

A colleague of mine tells this story. During a particulary stressful time while she was working on her Ph.D. dissertation, she became sick and went to the university clinic for medical care. When the nurse questioned her about the problem, my colleague spontaneously burst into tears.

The nurse's response was: "Well, now. Crying won't help, will it?"

The nurse did not turn inside and describe what she was feeling, thinking or wanting. She focused outside. As a result, I infer she wanted my colleague to stop crying, not for my colleague's sake, but to relieve her own internal discomfort. "Crying won't help" really meant, "I'm uncomfortable."

As a result, my colleague's stress increased. Not only was she sick, it became her job to help the helper.

You will shift from managing others to managing yourself with others.

Once you recognize how people need others outside to change what they feel inside, you'll begin to notice it every-where. Folks continually need others to do their own inside work.

This is good reason to recognize and be in charge of what is inside you. Believe me, there is no shortage of folks who seek to make their inside virtual reality stories better by work-ing to get you to change yours. Without the slightest effort, you can find yourself being a feast for the famished.

You Don't Know What You Don't Know

You know whether or not you can perform calculus. You know whether you can drive a car, hit a golf ball, fly a plane or grow wheat. You know whether you understand the relationship of the tilt of the Earth to the seasons and to the weather. If you don't know, you know where to get the information.

Think of learning from others as a very personal scientific endeavor. Just as there was a time when people didn't know what caused the change of seasons (but *thought* they did), you may assume you know some things about yourself and others when you don't. Learning from others is a process of gathering information that will enable you to modify your reality or internal stories to better reflect the truth.

The search for real information from others is science. However, in learning from the inside–out, you are both the subject *and* the scientist. Like other scientists, your task is to describe what you know, and inquire about what is mystery. You describe your feelings, intentions and judgments, and inquire from others about their intentions, assumptions, expectations and feelings. This data is critical to fully understand what's happening in the present with another person.

Once you've gathered this information, you can compose a picture that is much more complete and accurate than your unresearched story. When you create this more robust version of what's true in a particular situation, you'll make choices that are based on truth and less on your own internal imaginings. You can have purposeful, useful dialogue with others that moves projects forward. *Without scientific inquiry into what's really so and its accompanying information exchange, there is no learning; therefore, there is no way to discover what's true about anything.*

Whose Life is This Anyhow?

When you do what comes naturally, you often think the facts and problems are "out there." You can then comfortably

> *Without scientific inquiry into what's true, there is no learning; therefore, there is no way to discover what's true about anything.*

blame others (or the elevator), but you give up being the author of your life.

When you see that the other exists *in you*, you begin to take responsibility for your perceptions—for what you "know" and how you know it, and for the way you see others and the world. You begin to act as the creator of your experience.

You give each event, person, and interaction meaning and context. You attach one feeling or another to interactions; and you determine what a particular conversation means in the overall context of your life. *When you accept the responsibility for creating your own experience, you also take responsibility for how you respond to that experience.*

So, as Pogo once wisely said, "I have seen the enemy and he is us." Our one alternative is to learn.

When you accept responsibility for the creation of your experience, you also take responsibility for your response.

Short Takes

- ■ Recognize that what you think is "reality" is largely your own creation—then have the courage to own it.
- ■ Accept that others' internal "virtual reality" is real to them.
- ■ Welcome the discrepancies between these two "realities" as an opportunity to learn—to be both scientist and subject.
- ■ Be open to new choices available to you so you can alter what you have accepted as real.

Exercise

1. On a blank sheet of paper, write down one judgment that you have about the person you selected. Ask yourself where that judgment originates—from the other or you?
2. Write a judgment you *believe* the other person has of you. Where does that judgment originate? From the other or you?

3. Check your understanding. If you recognize both of the above come from you, you *understand* the lesson. If you personally feel responsible for creating those judgments, you are *living* the lesson.

    If you are now curious about you and the other person, you're ready to move on. Congratulations!

Thinking Lesson 4
LEARNING FROM INSIDE–OUT

> **In this lesson you'll discover that you learn not from changing for others or having others change for you, but by being true to who you really are.**
> **This lesson is about integrity and authenticity.**

Our plot thickens now because learning takes two people, both of whom are composing stories about the other. While you attribute intentions, motives and feelings to the other, the other returns the favor. You both often react to what, in *your* head, you assume is going on in the *other* person's head.

So, do you understand the dilemma? We now have two people living in the other's head instead of their own. Both can think they are interacting, while they are simply hearing the echo of their own stories.

The solution is to separate the stories—to have differentiated interactions.

You create differentiated interactions when you and the other person share from the inside–out what is real to you in the here and now. It is called "differentiated" because the process clearly separates your internal story from the other's.

For example, Person A has tears in his eyes. Person B's story about A is that A is depressed. Person B is concerned. What happens next makes all the difference.

To be differentiated is to share from the inside–out what is real to us.

Undifferentiated

Person B: "Hey guy. Take some time off. Get out of here for a while. Take care of yourself. Relax."

Differentiated

Person B: "I'm concerned that you are crying. Can I help?"

The second differentiated comment provides information on the speaker's internal state and asks for information, which proves to be a useful thing to do, given A's response:

Person A: "No. I have an allergy. The ragweed is bad this year."

Being undifferentiated means that you assume you know what is inside the other. This leads to some common, but very strange behaviors.

Which of the following are your favorites?

❏ Do something to others because you "know" that they will do something to you.

❏ Decide to do something because you "assume" the other wants you to.

❏ Give the other information you're "sure" he or she wants to hear.

❏ Talk with a third party about what you're "sure" the original person doesn't want to hear.

❏ Get others to change when you need to change.

❏ Make judgments about others which are judgments you have about yourself.

❏ Attribute motives to others which are your own.

❏ Attribute feelings to others which you have toward them.

❏ Accuse others of doing unto to you what you are doing to them.

Differentiated interactions make clear who is the author of what story.

But what does it mean to be a differentiated individual human being? *It means having the ability to be an 'I' in the face of 'we' pressures.*[*] It requires:

- an awareness and ownership of your own internal state;
- a willingness to share your internal state with others as information (not as a statement about external reality, but rather as a statement about *your* internal reality);
- the ability to say what's true for you, in spite of the pressure to do otherwise;
- the ability to stay in contact and in relationship with others, and to listen, understand and be open to influence from their positions; and
- the courage to be true to your own way of seeing things.

Being differentiated means being secure enough in yourself to stand your ground while being open to others, to the possibility of change and to the power of choice. It does not mean to push away in order to be yourself. It doesn't mean "I'm out a' here. You can't fire me. I quit!" It also doesn't mean "You're absolutely right. I'm wrong."

Having said that, I agree that differentiation is a wonderful goal, but my belief is that being differentiated is a *state,* and a rather saintly one at that. Because our focus is on learning, I am more interested in differentiation as a process or activity that brings clarity and new information. My emphasis here is to create differentiated *interactions.* Over time, this is one of many paths to individual differentiation.

To participate in a differentiated interaction means to describe what is truly going on inside—even if it is undifferentiated and fused.

> *Differentiated interactions make clear who is the author of what story.*

[*] Edwin Friedman, 1985.

To return to my earlier example:

Person B: "Your tears really effect me. They make me sad and cry for you too—and (sob) I don't have the foggiest idea why."

A differentiated interaction is being able to say "I'm unclear right now. I don't know what is going on. I couldn't find my opinion or a feeling if I had a butterfly net."

Once you learn the differences between undifferentiated and differentiated interactions, you'll see undifferentiated conversations everywhere, in every encounter, in every meeting. You'll see the incredible amount of time wasted when people talk about "it," and argue about "they" and "it" when "it" and "they" aren't the relevant topic. However, individual beliefs, intentions and feelings about "it" and "they" are relevant.

I'll use a conversation with my daughter, Sarah, to illustrate.

A few years ago, I was watching the Seattle Seahawks on television in their last pre–season football game. The fans were testing a new "noise" rule that penalized the home team if the crowd was too loud for the opposing players to hear.

The crowd was deafening. The Seahawks were penalized, but of course this did not stop the noise; it became the reason for more. The crowd, not to be dictated to by some "dumb" rule, became louder. The game could not go on. The Seahawks were penalized again. And again. And again. The noise simply got as loud as possible and remained there. I was having a delightful time.

At this point, Sarah very quietly said: "Football is boring."

Ron: "What! It's *not* boring. How can you say it's boring? Look at the noise meter!"

Sarah: "Well, it just *is* boring."

> *To participate in a differentiated interaction means to describe what is truly inside you, even if it is undifferentiated.*

38

Ron: (now playfully) "If *it* is so boring, why are so many people excited? How can 60,000 loyal, true, reverent, red–blooded Americans be wrong? Just look at that crowd!"

Sarah: (joining in the fun) "I don't care. *It* still *is* boring!"

Ron: "No, it's not!"

Sarah: "It is too."

Because we were talking about football and not interacting from the inside–out, we participated in an undifferentiated interaction. I did not know what was in her head, but assumed I did. She didn't know what was in my head, but assumed she did.

It was fun for a while, but because my focus was outside on the other, I gradually made up different stories, these not so pleasant. She became "intrusive and obstinant."
I tried to keep my sense of humor, but now, I have to confess, it had a slight bite.

Ron: "You know, you really are judgmental. I've been wanting to talk to you about that." (With a hopeful ha, ha.)
This apparently miffed Sarah. She's quick.

Sarah: "You're the one who's calling me judgmental? I suppose you don't call that being judgmental?"

Because we really disagreed, it became even more undifferentiated. As it seems to always happen in undifferentiated interactions—one *it* (football), changed to another *it* (you).

At this stage, our internal states (what we each thought, felt and wanted) were pasted onto each other. I was frustrated because she was upset. She didn't have a right to get upset with me just because I was upset. Naturally that upset me. Wouldn't it upset you? She was upset just because she thought I was upset with her, thinking that she is a judgmental human being. Now that's undifferentiated!

39

You can see why we didn't learn. Neither of us shared real information. Football wasn't the appropriate topic. Our stories *about* football and each other were.

The only way to learn was to talk to each other from the inside–out, describe our stories and inquire about the other's story.

Ron: "Hey Sarah, let's stop this and talk about what's going on with each of us. I want to learn. I'm irritated and confused. Are you upset with me?"

Sarah: "Yes, I guess I am. Right from the beginning when I expressed that I didn't like football, you ignored me. I didn't think you were paying any attention to me."

Ron: "I sure didn't think you were serious. I thought you were playing."

Sarah: "I guess I was being playful. That's because it's hard for me to talk to you about how much television time football takes up . . ."

We created a differentiated interaction. We shared information and we learned.

In undifferentiated interactions, we make our *stories, judgments and feelings* stick to objects. We walk around with an infinite supply of Post–it Notes to put "out there" on whatever exists. Sarah's Post–it Note for football was "boring," mine was "exciting." Football *is* boring and *is* exciting. Since both Sarah and I believed that our notes were actual attributes of what was outside (football) and not what was inside (how we felt right then), we differed and argued.

This kind of interaction leads us to do the only reasonable thing—paste Post–it Notes on each other. Now, instead of *it* being boring or exciting, we can argue about the other being "intrusive," "obstinate" or "insensitive (or whatever we wish to

> *In undifferentiated interactions, we make our stories stick to others. . . like Post–it notes.*

project) without revealing what is inside each of us that drives those judgments.

By the time we're face to face and attempting to learn, I'm covered with your stickers and you're covered with mine. By looking inside and describing our stories, we can take back the Post-its from each other and, at least, get a glimpse of what is mine, what is yours, and what is *true* about each of us.

Short Takes

■ Differentiated interactions are the key to learning from others.

■ To look inside at what is real separates or differentiates you from the other.

■ To share from the inside–out creates differentiated interactions.

■ Differentiated interactions do not come from being differentiated, but from being true to who you are in the moment.

Exercise

(5) Always
(4) Frequently
(3) Occasionally
(2) Seldom
(1) Never

1. Use the above scale and rate each of the questions below. Think of your interactions with your selected person. To what degree have you turned inside and:

_____Described what you want?

_____Described what you feel?

_____Checked out your attributions? Your judgments?

_____Inquired about what the other person wants and feels?

2. Think of what you would say to begin a differentiated interaction.

3. Check your understanding.

If you now feel challenged, not to change yourself or the other, but to *be* more true to your story and curious about the story the other has of you, you've got the essence of this lesson. Congratulations!

Thinking Lesson 5
LEARNING FROM PATTERNS

In this lesson, you'll learn that you can take your awareness of what is inside you and others, step back, observe patterns and simplify.

Understanding patterns provides a map for seeing and choosing differentiated learning patterns.

Given that all patterns are co–created, this lesson will relieve you from the twin burdens of innocence and blame.

Up to this point, the lessons have put you in the middle, to look, live and learn from the inside-out, and to uncover and discover here–and–now information. All lessons have emphasized a turn from the outside to the inside in order to find and communicate information. This lesson is not about what is going on inside you at all. Rather, it is about learning from the overt, very public patterns of behavior that happen between and among you and others.

These simple patterns are among the most powerful sources of here–and–now information and learning that you can have.

Patterns

You and others have unconsciously agreed–upon, repetitive ways of acting in concert with each other. Together, you create patterns of behavior. Think of these patterns not as individual habits but as a dance which involves a minimum of two people. As you do what you do, the other acts in response to what you do, and vice versa. *Together* you create patterns.

If you don't speak to each other when upset, that is a pattern. If you talk to each other constantly, that is a pattern. If you talk business, that is a pattern. If you gossip, that is a pattern. The point is, as long as you are in an interdependent relationship, there is no way out. Whatever you do, or don't do, can be seen as a pattern. You are always dancing.

Patterns are inclusive of all that goes on in your organization, from work flow to establishing the annual budget, how you resolve interpersonal disagreements to how you are greeted in the morning. Everything that happens in an organization or group, if it happens repetitively, is a pattern.

Every relationship you have is structured by your here–and–now patterns of interaction. When you achieve your goals, the patterns are effective. When you are unable to meet your goals, the patterns are ineffective.

Patterns are neither good nor bad. They simply are.

Everything that happens in an organization or group is a pattern if it happens repetitively.

Patterns are Co–Created

As I mentioned in the introduction, "individuals or groups, *not their interactions*, get the blame (for what goes wrong in organizations). This very predictable human reflex blocks information and prevents learning." Which individual would you hold accountable for the following interaction?

Mary: "I told your department that I needed this information a week ago."

Ted: "Well, nobody told me. I just heard about it Monday, and I can't just drop everything at a moment's notice."

Without knowing any more than this, you can detect, at the simplest level of analysis, the pattern. Mary blames; Ted explains and defends.

44

Who is responsible for the pattern? Mary blames *because* Ted explains. Ted explains *because* Mary blames. Where we pin the tail of cause is merely a matter of arbitrary punctuation. Causation is circular. Both of them create and maintain the pattern.

Any patterns you and your colleagues have are created by all of you. You are all active, card–carrying members who help to maintain them. However, this is often difficult to detect because of your out–there, outside, other–focus. It is far easier to see the other's behavior than to notice how your behavior invites the other's behavior, and thus co–creates the pattern.

Recognizing patterns means saying goodbye to both innocence and blame.

Patterns Maintain Themselves

A few years ago I wanted to study interactions, so I watched videotapes of groups we were training. After the first few tapes, I became bored. Thanks to the "FF" button, I discovered why I was bored.

I could watch the first minute or so of group interaction, fast forward to the end of the tape, and see that even though the participants had changed topics, they talked to each other in the same way as in the beginning. Their patterns of interaction were the same over time and operated regardless of the topic.

My job suddenly became less onerous. All I had to do was watch the first few minutes and capture how the group functioned. (Saved a lot of time, not to mention the wear and tear of boredom.)

As a consultant, I typically see patterns that chug along and do their thing, even though every individual I interview doesn't want or like them. If we miss a pattern that doesn't work the first time around, don't worry; it will still be detectable on the 551st time it comes around.

To recognize patterns means to say goodbye to both innocence and blame.

All interactions create patterns. Again, patterns are neither good nor bad, they simply exist. The only way to determine their value is whether they meet your purpose or your goal. If the purpose of a meeting is to disseminate information, that calls for one kind of pattern. If the goal is to have high participation and involvement, that calls for a different pattern. If you are brainstorming or making decisions, different patterns are required for each.

Patterns serve purposes, sometimes conscious, mostly unconcious. Sometimes they serve a purpose that has a high degree of emotional charge. Often, you will discover the purpose only after you change the patterns.

Patterns serve a purpose, sometimes conscious, mostly unconscious.

Patterns Simplify

After watching literally hundreds of teams communicate, I'm convinced that for most organizational purposes, people make interactions far more complex than they need to be. In fact, the more I'm around organizations, teams and groups, the more I believe there are very few patterns which typically occur in work conversations. We could probably count them on the fingers of both hands. (I briefly describe seven of the most common non–learning patterns on pages 103 to 105.)

As you practice observing patterns, you will find that they can be categorized rather easily and simply. If you listen very simply to the patter of interaction, you can know what a partnership looks and sounds like, regardless of the topic, and whether it is between customer and supplier, boss and subordinate, or peers. You'll recognize the patterns of communication in meetings and how they keep you from accomplishing your goals. You'll know from the patter of the pattern whether a disagreement is going to lead anywhere.

To simplify further, for our purposes there are only two kinds of patterns—those that differentiate and lead to learning, and those that are undifferentiated and do not lead to learning. In Part 2, Inquiry Lessons, we'll examine them in greater detail.

Short Takes

- One key to learning from others is to see yourself as a participant in the creation and maintenance of patterns.

- Changing patterns is simple to understand and difficult to do.

- When patterns support your ability to achieve your goals, they are effective; when they don't, they're not.

- The problem, therefore, is often not the stated problem but *the underlying patterns that keep the stated problem in place.*

Exercise

1. Think about the typical patterns of interaction between you and your selected person. What does the other person actually do? What do you do?

2. Can you think of an adjective that characterizes your typical "dance?"

3. Check your understanding.

   If you can let go of *what* you and the other person say to each other and observe at the simplest level *how* both of you say it, then you understand the lesson.

   If you are challenged to learn to identify the dance *while* it is happening, you are ready to use this lesson. Congratulations!

   The previous lessons have one assumption in common. *All the information you require to learn from each other is always present, all the time, in every situation, within, among and between you and the others involved, in the here and now.*

There are only two kinds of patterns— those that differentiate and lead to learning, and those that are undifferentiated and do not lead to learning.

Therefore, the next and final lesson is about the essential ability to use this information. It is the capacity to be present, to become aware, observe and notice what is inside and outside of you in the moment, in the here and now.

Thinking Lesson 6
NOTICING NOW

> **All learning requires that you be aware, notice and observe *now*. Awareness gives you the ability to choose now.**
>
> **Your observer provides that awareness.**

This final thinking lesson focuses on how to observe and learn from what is going on right here and now.

There is a great deal of talk today about "using yourself," "being authentic," and "leading with yourself." That has been my goal. However you may discover as I have that often when I thought I was being my authentic self, I was not. Instead, I was being *reactive*. (See pp. 118–120.)

The secret to learning is to *observe*, not *change*, yourself.

As you'll learn in Inquiry Lesson 2 about mutual inquiry, when you interact from the inside–out, you describe yourself. You do not change yourself into someone else, but describe who you truly are in the moment. Also, you do not change others but invite them to be who they truly are with you, right now in the moment. *Information about your separate stories changes the relationship, not the individuals in the relationship.*

Your Observer

The key to learning is to be as aware as possible of what is *now*. You have that ability through your elusive and invisible observer, a function of your "Self." There are many ways to talk about your Self—actor, object, subject, the private you, the adaptive you, the real you, the ideal you—but your Self is all of these and more. Your Self is all of the activities that you call yourself.

Because the ability to be present in the *now* is what concerns us here, we will focus on your Self as observer. It is your here–and–now witness. Your observer notices you and what you think, feel and want. When activated it observes your behavior and the story going on inside you in the moment.

Your observer is tricky because by the time you notice it's there, it has already moved on to observe you noticing. You can never catch it with language, because once you name something, the observer is gone and notices that you're naming.

Your observer is not an object that can be described. It is not what you feel or think. It is not even your observations. Rather, your observer is the function that prompts you to say, "Hmmm, there I go again," or "How I'm being now is getting me nowhere," or "I may be interpreting his behavior all wrong," or "I'm simply stuck in this interaction doing the same thing over and over and over."

The observer is not your judgmental process—it's the process that *notices* when you judge. It's not the feeling you have—it's that part of you that *notices* you feel the feeling. It's not the part of you that needs and wants to be more differenti-ated—it's the part that *notices* how you're being and leads you to see that "I'm not at all differentiated right now." It's not the ability to control what happens to you but the ability to *observe* how you respond to what happens. It's not the process of debriefing what happens, it's what pops up *while* you are debriefing and *notices* how you are debriefing.

Your observer is quick! You can never capture it, but you can train yourself to pause long enough to activate it. You

When activated, your observer notices your behavior and the story going on inside you in the moment.

50

can identify when your elusive observer is active by three characteristics:

1. It always *observes in the present.* You can't *notice* in the past; you can only remember.

2. It always *observes the Self.*

3. It always *observes without judgment*; it simply notices that you are judging.

The more you use your observer, the smarter it gets. Over time it knows what to look for because it has learned your patterns. Your observer gives you choice because it notices what you are doing so you can say, "Hmmm. . .there I go again."

Your Observer as Your Immune System

Reactivity is contagious. Anxiety spreads faster than a bad cold and soon has everybody bouncing off the walls. The greater the emotional intensity in a situation, the more you need your observer.

You know that in order to learn, you need to share information. You know that information comes from differenti-ated interactions. You have the map, but the degree to which you can get there in any given intense moment is the degree to which your observer notices how reactive you are. *It is only this noticing that enables you to make different choices.* Essentially, your observer enables you to set boundaries between you and the intense emotional field.

You have the ability to become present to your observer and notice, "Yes, I feel this, and what I feel is real. But I need more information to determine what's *true*." Think of your observer as an immune system that enables you to step down the emotional intensity, not only for you but also for those around you. It allows you to pause, see what's so for you in the

The greater the emotional intensity in a situation, the more you need your observer.

moment, put on your scientist hat, and gather information so that you can learn rather than simply react.

This ability does not come easily. It is truly a challenge to learn, but is is important to accept the challenge because this ability to observe your Self enables you to turn non–learning, difficult interactions into learning.

Short Takes

■ Your observer notices you in the moment.

■ This information is the basis for choice, stepping down reactivity and learning.

■ Your observer enables you to see when you are not learning and to make a choice.

Exercise

1. On a blank sheet of paper, write an adjective that characterizes *you* when you interact with your chosen other.

2. As you write, notice if part of you observes yourself without judgment. If so, that is your observer.

   Whoops! Your observer has moved on to watch you read this. . .No, too late. . . now it's watching what's going on inside you as you read this paragraph. . .No, too late again. It's moved on. And on. . .

3. Check your understanding.

   If you are challenged to develop your ability to be present, to observe you and here–and–now patterns of behavior, you are prepared to move on to the Inquiry Lessons. Congratulations!

Part 2
Inquiry Lessons

All the information you require to learn from each other is always present

Inquiry Lessons

To begin **Inquiry Lessons**, think of yourself as immersed in the information you need to learn. This information is constantly present inside and outside of you in every interaction and relationship.

These lessons prepare you to uncover this here–and–now information from three vantage points.

1. *Learn From Among: Systems Inquiry.* From this big–picture perspective, you find the information in the structure, roles and underlying patterns among all of you.

2. *Learn From Between: Mutual Inquiry.* From this perspective, you engage face to face with another person to learn directly from each other from the inside–out.

3. *Learn From Within: Self Inquiry.* As you certainly know by now, much of the here–and–now information lies within you and is about you.

You can view every moment, every conversation, interaction and meeting from each of these three positions. As you gain skill, you'll shift from one to the other; discover how interdependent, interrelated and connected they are; and be able to choose which to use in any given circumstance to learn.

Part 3, Applications Lessons, gives you step–by–step methods you can use from each perspective.

Brad and Mary: An Example

To illustrate important points throughout the Inquiry Lessons, I want you to meet two fictional characters, Mary and Brad, both consultants and trainers who are often partnered to deliver training.

To learn from information that includes ourselves is the challenge we all face if we are to learn from different perspectives.

Mary and Brad have worked together for over a year with considerable success. Not only are they both excellent trainers, they discovered early on how they complement each other. Mary is the more intuitive of the two and is, therefore, able to give big–picture direction. She is the visionary, focusing on what is possible and sometimes dazzles participants with her gifts. Brad, on the other hand, is a natural at managing details. His focus is on what is real. He is the organizer, the person who can attend to the details necessary to make the trainings run smoothly. And furthermore, he loves doing it.

Together, Mary and Brad formed a great partnership—at least for a while.

Recently there have been some cues to Mary that something isn't right. Nothing big, just some little things like Brad not smiling or not saying good morning last Tuesday. Or how he looked away and didn't make eye contact when talking to her. Or how he just schlepps stuff around with his head down. Or that one time when he snapped at her when she innocently asked when she had to be at the next training event.

"He's getting an attitude. What a grump!"

The truth is, Brad has grown tired of his job. He's the one who carts stuff around. He wakes up at night sweating the details and makes sure that all the bases are covered. He is the one who has to remind Mary of things she needs to bring to the training. He's getting sick and tired of the burden and wants Mary to "be more responsible."

"I'm getting tired of babysitting."

Neither has talked to the other. Both want change. . . that is, the *other* to change.

These virtual realities have become so "real" that Mary did not acknowledge it when Brad smiled at her the other day.

His smile "was sarcastic." Brad was actually irritated when Mary offered to help him. "She should *not* help *him* do *her* job. It's *her* job, too."

Mary and Brad are trapping themselves.

Let's use the knowledge from the three perspectives to understand how they are stuck and see whether they use it to learn from each other.

Inquiry Lesson 1
LEARNING FROM AMONG: SYSTEMS INQUIRY

Inquiry Lesson 1 pulls you away from what is inside you (the focus so far) to look at the context and the behavioral patterns that you help create and sustain which are outside you.

The reason for this change is simple. First, much of what you observe going on in you in relationship is often the *result* of the context and patterns—not the cause. Often you can change your patterns in response and discover that what you feel and think inside about other folks has changed as a result. As you become aware of yourself participating in the same patterns over and over, it is inevitable that you will ask how you contribute to the pattern and why you continue to do what you do.

Learning from behavioral patterns is a window into learning about yourself.

Examining your patterns may require you to dramatically shift how you think, but the results will be well worth it. Understanding your patterns and how you maintain them are the most powerful and empowering tools you can have. When your organization or team is stuck, look first at patterns. When you have a problem with another individual, make a stop here first. When you feel crazy at work, look here first because if you're in a crazy system, you'll feel crazy—especially if you are not.

This lesson provides the central ideas—structure, boundaries and change. These fundamental theoretical lessons will help you use the techniques in Part 3, Application Lessons.

To learn from others, much of what you need to know is among you right here and right now.

Key Concepts

Structure

To work effectively, every system needs a structure to which all participants agree. This *formal* structure helps you coordinate with others and meet your goals. It includes the roles and methods to solve problems, make decisions, run meetings, be part of a self–managed team, create and manage organizational change, or whatever you are attempting to achieve.

The structure we are concerned with is what emerges even while you are planning a more formal structure.

The structure this lesson focuses on is more fundamental and emerges *while* you implement the formal structures. The focus is on patterns of interaction that underlie, support, or sabotage formally agreed–upon structures.

Patterns of interaction establish the *real* structure, regardless of organizational wiring, job descriptions, or role descriptions. In other words, you can collectively agree on a structure, define who will do what for what reasons and then the *real, fundamental* structure emerges *while* you do the work. For example, you can agree:

- who will make the decision—then interact in ways that defy even Superwoman's ability to make the decision;
- how to resolve conflict openly and honestly—then sweep conflict and disagreement under the rug;
- who will be the leader—then coalesce to render him or her totally ineffective;
- to treat your clients as customers—then sell them something they didn't ask for and don't need; or
- to be partners—then partner with others against your declared partner.

I could give more illustrations, but I hope the distinction is clear. The structure we are concerned with is what emerges even while you are planning a more formal structure. You become organized *while* you are planning how you will organize. This real and more fundamental structure is always going on; and these here–and–now patterns of behavior can be more permanent, more powerful and determining than any formal agreed–upon organizational structure.

Brad and Mary

If you look at the organization chart, Mary and Brad are peers. They both report to Susan, the executive director. They have also agreed upon how they will work together—who is responsible for what, how they will make decisions, etc.

In the meantime, while working in these explicit formal structures, they have created the informal, more fundamental structure that is giving them fits. That is, Brad carts stuff around around, Mary seems to flit.

Multiple Structures

You participate in multiple systems many times a day, often with the same people. Each occasion requires appropriate, here–and–now structures to achieve your objectives. This may appear to make things more complex, but hang in there. As you'll see later, this is one huge step toward simplification.

Your system not only changes with different people, it changes with the same people when you converse about different topics.

Every relationship you have constitutes a different system. Add someone to a relationship and you have another system. Add more, and it is yet another system. Then, (this is critical information) *your system not only changes with different people, it changes when the same people converse about different topics.*

For instance, you have a colleague who is also a friend. You play golf together and talk about personal issues. That is one system. However, when the two of you talk about business, you are immediately in different roles, which is another system. When you and your colleagues discuss the budget, that is one system. When you brainstorm ideas, that is yet another. Different roles; different system.

Think of yourself as flipping and flopping in and out of systems from moment to moment. Each time your system changes with people or different topics, the structure of roles, as well as patterns, also change.

Whew! This doesn't sound simple does it?

It is simple because—and here comes the idea that is so useful—*major problems arise when one system interferes with another.* Some examples are:

Problems arise when one system interferes with another.

- you talk only about business with your spouse, never about your relationship;

- your team talks about vacations when a touchy personnel issue is on the agenda;

- the owners of a family–owned business work to solve a business problem at the Christmas party;

- the son in a family–owned business states that he can goof off as much as he wants because his Mom and Dad can't fire a family member;

- you discuss an important business issue in the midst of interruptions; or

- the owners of an organization interfere with the person they designated to manage it.

A marriage is one system which requires one kind of structure; a business is another. The family–owned business Christmas party is one system; solving a business problem is another. The boss (father or mother) of the family–owned business clearly needs to be able to hold the employee (the son) accountable and also be "parents" outside of work. Business meetings need to be conducted without interruptions. A manager needs to manage without interference from the owners.

Brad and Mary

Their problem is growing because their patterns in one system (organizing the training) are interfering with another system (delivering effective training). Also, because they do not interact directly they are violating each other's boundaries by attributing negative motives to each other.

All the above examples illustrate systems which, in order to learn, must be protected from interference. How do you keep one system from interfering with another? Boundaries.

Boundaries

The function of a boundary is to protect one system from interference by another. Formal, explicit structures basically establish boundaries. Clarity about purpose and roles constitute boundaries. Defining who has the authority establishes a boundary.

This entire book is a lesson in boundaries. You create learning and differentiate with boundaries. When you are aware of your internal experience, you create a boundary. When you interact from the inside–out, you create a boundary that says "this is me, that is you." As you'll learn later, descriptive (as opposed to reactive) language creates boundaries. You create boundaries when you take responsibility for what is inside you.

Boundaries (and lack of them) exist everywhere, in every circumstance, and every conversation. We often miss the power boundaries have on our lives. Like a virus that penetrates a cell membrane, when boundaries are violated the effect can be devastating—even when we do not see or understand why.

If you change what you feel, want and think because you *think* others want you to do that, you violate your boundaries. When someone tells you what you *should* feel or believe, rather than listen to what you *do, in fact*, feel and believe, he or she violates your boundaries. When someone implies or tells

The function of a boundary is to protect one system from interference from another system.

63

you directly what your motive is for doing something, he or she violates your boundaries. When someone talks *about* you rather than *to* you, he or she violates a boundary.

Therefore, think boundary. This is fundamental to every human relationship. Without boundaries you have unclear, contaminated, distorted information—no boundaries, no clarity; no clarity, no learning.

Change

Action, not understanding, creates change.

Change only happens when something changes. Action, not understanding, creates change. You can know your team avoids disagreement and you can understand why, but change and learning do not occur until someone disagrees. You can collectively agree that you have ineffective meetings and you can understand why, but change and learning only happen when you act differently in meetings.

So, if communication is a problem, communicate. If important boundaries are violated, say no. If leadership is a problem, lead. If decisions are a problem, decide. If you want to be listened to, listen. If you want a learning culture, learn.

This latter is said simply, but is often anything but that. When you try to change a pattern alone, just get ready for reactions and patterns that attempt to force you back into the old, the familiar.

Some will come from within you.

Brad and Mary

Brad could break the pattern simply by not doing what he's always done. However, (and this is what goes on in his head when he thinks about it), "That would drive me crazy; the training would fail; we'd get a negative evaluation; I'd be fired; lose my house and my wife; my kids couldn't go to college. Better just keep schlepping."

Many reactions will, without question, come from others. Mary will not want Brad to change. Their boss will be very concerned, and on and on.

I have seen one example over and over again. Many teams and organizations strive to break the old authoritarian, command–and–control patterns by establishing new, even more coercive structures. The pattern shifts from one person making all the decisions to nobody making any. They now think everything has to be decided by everybody. Or they shift from no team meetings to spending so much time in ineffective meetings that no other work gets done.

Learning does not occur because when someone finally finds the courage to initiate leadership and point out the problem, morality is often invoked: "Be a team player, we're a participatory organization." This really means: "Fall back in line. Participate, but don't participate *that* way."

Short Takes

- Structure is fundamental.
- The formal, agreed–upon structure of rules, roles and goals needs to be supported by the informal structure; that is, the repetitive patterns of here–and–now interaction.
- You are in multiple systems depending on who is present, the topic and the purpose.
- Boundaries keep one system from interference from another.
- Without boundaries there is no clarity—no clarity, no learning.
- Action, not understanding, creates change and learning.

Inquiry Lesson 2
LEARNING FROM BETWEEN: MUTUAL INQUIRY

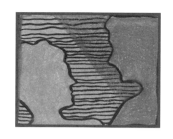

This perspective places you face to face with another person—seeking to learn, to clear up misunderstandings, misinterpretations and misattributions. Simply put, it is the process that two people must inevitably use, either intentionally or not, to complete an interaction where the outcome is understanding each other.

This is the most important lesson in this book. I used to wonder how to understand and be understood by someone else. I used to wonder how I could correct a frustrating interaction that had gone south—what I needed to do to build and maintain trust—what made the difference between a mumbling, muttering, messed up group and a dynamic team. I used to wonder what would help some groups that appeared to be open, but talked and talked endlessly about their feelings and yet got nowhere, frustrating everybody.

I now know what makes the difference. It lies in whether the individuals involved talk directly to each other, capably engage in mutual inquiry and learn.

Perhaps life has already taught you the essence of this lesson. Once I trained a group of managers and noticed an uncommonly skilled participant. He was a model for others. Curious, I pulled him aside during a break to give him positive feedback and find out where he learned the skills.

Ron: "I am impressed with your abilities. You must have had a lot of training in these ideas and skills."

Participant: (cynically) "Yeah, I've had training. I went through a long, tough divorce."

To learn from others, much of what you need to know is between you and one other person—right here and right now.

Not only is mutual inquiry important in the workplace, you'll find that it applies to all areas of your life. Mutual inquiry skill and awareness are the keys to learning relationships, regardless of your role.

In this lesson you'll learn the goal, the underlying dynamic, the role of language, what the process looks like, how you can trick yourself and be tricked, and the difference between being open and being personal.

Key Concepts

The goal of mutual inquiry is to learn what is true.

The Goal: Why Mutual Inquiry?

Engaging in mutual inquiry is not about how to save a relationship gone sour, although you'll find many of your relationships may improve; it is not to change another person, although that person may change *in your eyes*. The goal of mutual inquiry is not to change yourself, although you may find yourself changed. Mutual inquiry does not make all your relationships hum perfectly or resolve all your difficulties.

Mutual inquiry is, at its core, a method to learn what is true––about you, about the other person, and about your relationship now. Both you and the other may then find yourselves making more informed choices and, therefore, improving your relationship.

The goal is to learn. Keep this in mind because there are no guarantees. No matter how skilled and competent *you* are, mutual inquiry can fail because there is another person involved. By definition, you cannot do it alone. You can only take care of your side. Some may refuse to try. Others may use it as an opportunity to win, not to learn. And a very few are simply not capable of learning, regardless of how proficient *you* are.

You may not be able to learn with a particular person, but you can *always* learn about yourself.

The Underlying Dynamic

The most important element to bring to a mutual inquiry is not technique, or even skill, but curiosity and an understanding of underlying principles which the techniques and skills support. If you use the principles as a map and know where you are going, you'll find your way to get there.

Let's review and simplify the principles involved in learning from direct dialogue with another person.

Remember, your interpersonal world consists of only two, count 'em, *two*, orientations and each has its own language:

1. What is outside. This is dominant and reflexive. It demands that you address others from the outside–in.

2. What is inside. This is learned; it is subtle, tricky, and difficult. It invites you to engage with others from the inside–out.

Can anything be simpler than that? You've got a right and left. You've got an up and a down. You also have an inside and an outside.

As explained in Thinking Lesson 2, your experience in these two realities is like night and day. The outcomes of thinking from the outside versus the inside are 180 degrees apart. The focus from the outside–in does *not* lead to learning. It tends to create defensiveness, helplessness and resentment.

On the other hand, to successfully engage from the inside–out leads to mutual learning.

Although mutual inquiry almost invariably starts outside–in, if successful, it ends up with two people engaged with each other from the inside–out. Both parties learn about the other and themselves.

This means that you and the other person:

- separate what you *think* the other person feels from what the other person *reports* he or she feels;

Mutual inquiry happens when you search for and share descriptive information. Descriptive information is not arguable.

■ separate what you *think* are the other person's intentions from what he or she *reports* they truly are; and

■ separate what the other person actually *did* from your *interpretation* of his or her behavior and the impact it had on you.

Brad and Mary

Brad: "I'm getting tired of babysitting. Mary's turned into a user."

Mary: "Brad's sure getting an attitude. What a grump!"

"He's getting an attitude."

Simple enough? I'm sure you would agree that Brad needs to separate the story he's made up about Mary from the real Mary and her behavior. "She's a user," is probably very different from Mary's motivation and certainly different from Mary's internal view of herself. Brad's virtual reality (his feelings, values, beliefs, meanings, and desires) originates from and resides inside himself, not outside him in Mary.

Likewise, Mary needs to recognize that "grump" originates inside her. It is the way she interprets Brad's behavior.

Making the shift from outside–in to inside-out is profound. When mutual inquiry is conducted successfully, it results in far more than a simple change in language. Mutual inquiry takes both people through the "looking glass." What you thought was his or hers is actually yours. What you thought was outside in the other, you find inside yourself.

The Role of Language

Inside–out language begins with the pronoun "I." It describes what is inside you here and now. Other–focused language refers to "it," "one," "they," "he", or "she." It refers to an outside object or person, and tends to communicate more permanence and leaves you out. Here are some examples:

Outside Language	Inside Language
It is a beautiful day.	*I* feel energized and excited.
It's a stupid day!	*I'm* disgusted with myself.
You're a great artist.	*I* love this painting.
You're reckless!	*I'm* afraid of an an accident.
He's incompetent.	*I'm* frustrated and need help.
She's slow.	*I'm* impatient.

Compare the two realities and experience the difference. Dominant outside–object language places everything that happens *out there*, outside of you and totally independent of you. This makes you a passive spectator, even a nonentity who is "done unto" or acted upon by whatever is outside.

Inside language, however, describes what goes on *in* you. It places you in the center of the situation.

This shift takes you from passive victim to creator.

Outside language is arguable; inside language is not. Inside language states what is real and unarguable; outside language states conjectures and inferences.

Finally, inside language is *now* and temporary; outside language is judgmental and permanent.

Mutual inquiry makes the transition from the dominant object, "done–unto" victim reality to inside–self, "doing–unto" creator reality. Inside–self language makes you aware, responsible and leads to informed choice.

Inside language describes what goes on in you; it places you in the center of the situation.

The Process

Mutual inquiry takes place when two people create a dialogue that:

- closes the gap between intentions and impact;
- clarifies misunderstandings;

■ clarifies incorrect attributions; and

■ leads to mutual understanding.

To conduct mutual inquiry, you need two sets of skills— one set gives you information, the other invites and receives information. You *give* information by describing your here–and–now feelings, thoughts and wants. You *receive* information by listening and accepting the other person's internal feelings, thoughts and wants. With both people involved, it is a dance.

To successfully engage from the inside–out leads to mutual learning.

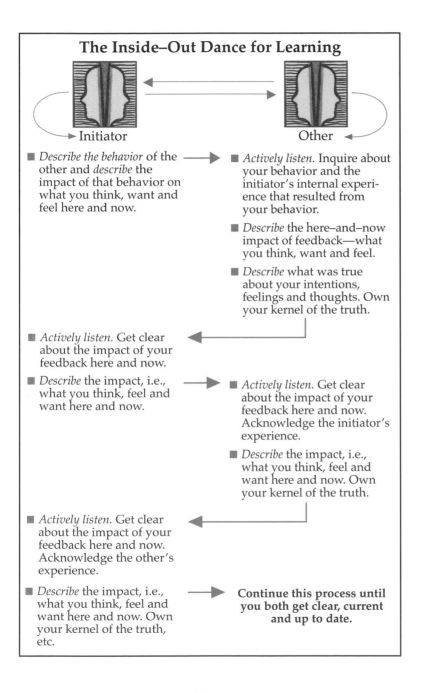

The Inside–Out Dance for Learning

Initiator

- *Describe the behavior* of the other and *describe* the impact of that behavior on what you think, want and feel here and now.

- *Actively listen.* Get clear about the impact of your feedback here and now.

- *Describe* the impact, i.e., what you think, feel and want here and now.

- *Actively listen.* Get clear about the impact of your feedback here and now. Acknowledge the other's experience.

- *Describe* the impact, i.e., what you think, feel and want here and now. Own your kernel of the truth, etc.

Other

- *Actively listen.* Inquire about your behavior and the initiator's internal experience that resulted from your behavior.

- *Describe* the here–and–now impact of feedback—what you think, want and feel.

- *Describe* what was true about your intentions, feelings and thoughts. Own your kernel of the truth.

- *Actively listen.* Get clear about the impact of your feedback here and now. Acknowledge the initiator's experience.

- *Describe* the impact, i.e., what you think, feel and want here and now. Own your kernel of the truth.

Continue this process until you both get clear, current and up to date.

When Brad and Mary danced, it might look like this:

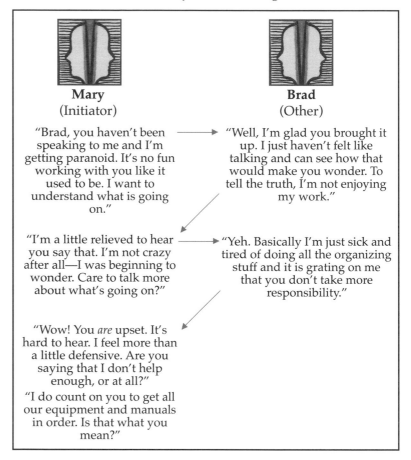

Mary
(Initiator)

"Brad, you haven't been speaking to me and I'm getting paranoid. It's no fun working with you like it used to be. I want to understand what is going on."

"I'm a little relieved to hear you say that. I'm not crazy after all—I was beginning to wonder. Care to talk more about what's going on?"

"Wow! You *are* upset. It's hard to hear. I feel more than a little defensive. Are you saying that I don't help enough, or at all?"

"I do count on you to get all our equipment and manuals in order. Is that what you mean?"

Brad
(Other)

"Well, I'm glad you brought it up. I just haven't felt like talking and can see how that would make you wonder. To tell the truth, I'm not enjoying my work."

"Yeh. Basically I'm just sick and tired of doing all the organizing stuff and it is grating on me that you don't take more responsibility."

Of course a real dialogue would be much longer, more convoluted, and possibly more heated. However, note the principle that Mary is sharing and seeking *information* which includes here–and–now feelings. She is sending a strong invitation to Brad to do the same.

When completed, Mary will understand Brad's frustration; Brad will understand Mary's intent; both Brad and Mary will know the impact their behavior has on the other and they will have a plan about what to do.

Tricking Ourselves

I continue to be amazed by my ability and the ability of others to trick ourselves and others. We can hang on to the "done–unto" reality even while using the correct language. Most of us have been taught to use "I" as opposed to "you" language to clarify interpersonal problems.

If you pay close attention to its popular usage, however, "I" language is often used to get the outside–other–object to change. The unstated assumption often is: *if* I use "I" language, *then you* will understand me, or change your opinion or whatever. When you use "I" language to merely drive your point home more politely, or get the other to change, learning probably will *not* occur. Unless learning is the goal, "I" language may leave others more confused and wondering about themselves— "Why do I feel so rotten when the other person was just being so open and honest."

"I" language can be used as a more subtle, insidious and sophisticated means to defend or attack, rather than disclose and uncover information. What appears to be open is often smoke and mirrors that put the politically correct spin on things, but fundamentally defends and protects the speaker's outside–other–object, "done–unto" victim reality.

Mary: "What do you mean that I don't help? I work every bit as hard as you do."

The giveaway as to why this "I" language won't go anywhere? Mary is not describing herself.

In order for mutual learning to occur, "I" messages must:

- be based upon a clear intent and agreement to learn;
- lead to being *descriptive* of the behavior and what is inside the people involved; and
- lead to mutual ownership.

When you use "I" language to get another to change, learning will probably not occur.

To create learning, these criteria must be used in your most superficial, as well as your deepest and most profound interpersonal interactions. Whether your goal is to clarify intentions with a colleague, or clean up difficult history in a primary relationship, mutual inquiry inevitably leads back inside, to describing and learning about yourself.

Being Open and Being Personal

Recognizing the difference between being open and being personal has been extremely helpful to me over the years. It is a concept I learned from two of my mentors, John Wallen and Bob Crosby.

To conduct mutual inquiry you must be open but not necessarily personal.

Occasionally in my trainings, folks have resisted practicing the skills because they thought they were playing psychologist and "shrinking" each other. They feared that to engage from the inside–out was to reveal their private lives. They believed it forced them to be too personal.

This is why it is so important to recognize the difference between being open and being personal.

If you are *personal,* you tell others about your personal life— what you do, where you are from, how you live; about your marriage, kids, and the difficulties you have. They learn *about* you.

If you are *open,* you tell others about the impact they have on you here and now; what you think, feel and want in the moment. They learn *from* you.

Obviously to conduct mutual learning you must be open, not necessarily personal. In fact, you can tell stories about yourself, your history, your family, and use it as a defense against being open.

Short Takes

- You have two fundamental orientations with two languages and realities: one observes from the *outside–in*; the other from the *inside–out*.

- Both realities are always present, in every situation and with every person.

- Your dominant orientation (outside–in) and language focuses outside where others "do unto" you.

- Mutual inquiry moves you from the outside–in reality to the inside–out reality.

- Language, habit, and how you are "wired" make this transition difficult.

- You learn from others by being open, not necessarily personal.

Inquiry Lesson 3
LEARNING FROM WITHIN:
SELF–INQUIRY

This lesson is about looking within and learning from yourself. Makes sense doesn't it? After all, when you notice yourself engaging in the same patterns over and over again, and facing the same issues with different people, who's always there? You!

As you engage and learn from others, you'll inevitably have to learn about yourself. I learned about me as I struggled to write this book.

> *I now understand what my emotional commitment is all about. It's not true that I've been writing this book for a few months. I have been working on it all my personal and professional life.*

I finally put words to why the book was so important to me—why I felt such intensity and commitment. I discovered that to help people learn from each other is not only my professional career; it was my self–appointed "job" as a child. The intensity of my conscious here–and–now experience was shaped by events that took place in a child's mind a long time ago. Somewhere locked up in the cells of my body is a neurological pattern. It became conscious as I reflected on my struggle to write this book.

You have these patterns as well. The focus of this lesson is to help you learn from them. When you make a commitment to learn from your interactions and relationships, you inevitably open the door to learn from your past. You cannot help but meet, not others, but yourself.

We all look through a window that turns out to be a mirror.

To learn from others, much of what you need to know is within you, right here and now.

It is important to keep your eye on learning as the goal. You'll see that this is not a "self–help, fix–yourself" lesson, but another source of here–and–now information that will increase your awareness and strengthen your ability to learn from others.

This chapter prepares you to use the methods in Part 3. It covers the Goal, the Underlying Dynamic, Own Impact, and Becoming Aware of your Defenses.

Key Concepts

The Goal

The goal is to learn, not to change.

The goal is to learn, not to change. It is to increase your horizon of awareness, along with your range of informed choices. It is about using these choices to create differentiated learning relationships. If you approach these ideas as tools to change yourself, you become an object, a thing to "fix" because you are not who you think you *should* be, or you don't behave as you *should* behave, or feel what you *should* feel. The unstated message is that you, as an object, should be different.

A focus on what you *should be* blinds you to what you *are.*

Therefore, the goal is to expand and develop the capacity to activate your non–judgmental observer that simply notices what *is* true, not what should be true. "Hmmm, there you go again wanting to change yourself. Do you want to do that now?"

Let's face it, if change is your goal, you've got a tough job to do. Your Self—your unique responses to internal and external stimuli—is the most patterned, channeled, rutted, intransigent, deeply rooted, highly predictable, seriously habituated part of you.

The goal is to notice, not to change. It is to develop the awareness, acknowledgement and acceptance of what is true about you *now*. The more you notice, the more you catch yourself in your unique patterns. The more you learn about why, when and how you developed these patterns in the past, the more you will be able to be present here and now and make different choices.

And, by the way, you just may wake up someday and realize that by not trying to change, but making here–and–now choices differently, you have changed.

This lesson is not about how to fully understand your past. In fact that's impossible. You created your personal history just as you create your current experience. From the inside–out, everything is *now*. If you think about some past event, you think about it *now*. If you're emotionally reactive because of what happened to you earlier in life, you're reactive *now*. You create a portion of your past that explains and, in some way, fits into your current reality.

You create your personal history just as you create your current experience.

My personal history is every bit a here–and–now personal construct, as is my current reality. As I type these words at 10:28 a.m., I select, discard and create *now* what was *then*. What happened then is not the issue. What I do *now* with what I think happened to me then is the issue. I am running the projector of my past *and* acting in it.

This is a lesson in how to inquire inside when any of the following occur in a relationship or interaction:

- Your emotional intensity is far greater than what the situation calls for.
- You thoroughly like or thoroughly dislike someone.
- You have certain "favorite" feelings or "favorite" thoughts toward a category of folks.
- You suddenly experience emotion for no apparent reason.
- You must do something that frightens you.

The Underlying Dynamic

Your experience is not what happens to you, but what you do internally with what happens to you. You create your experience.

Everytime you interact with another person in any situation, you ascribe meaning—you want, and you have feelings. Your virtual reality goes on behind your eyes all the time, whether you know it or not. Much of your contemporary, here–and–now experience is organized by images based on what you learned much earlier in life.

Your family was the first organization to which you belonged. Your parents were your first leaders. Your formative images about most aspects of contemporary organizational life, such as authority, cooperation, competition, men, women, and roles, were formed in your early experiences and remain with you.

As you go through your daily conscious life, much of how you experience your family, friends, co–workers or boss today was molded in the mind of a child long ago.

I owe this awareness to a friend and colleague, David Erb. He came to our graduate program years ago to help students understand authority. Given my academic background and out–there–other orientation, I expected an intellectually stimulating discussion on authority—where it comes from, how it is given, and so forth. Instead, Dave asked students to identify the faculty members who triggered the most emotional energy in them. They were then to explain why they felt so intensely toward that faculty member.

The students identified people, events and situations from their pasts that stimulated emotional response to their selected faculty member.

When the students shared their associations with me, some of the roles I played were a "priest," "nun in a Catholic

Your experience is not what happens to you, but what you do internally with what happens to you.

82

grade school," "wonderful big brother," "sadistic big brother," "loving father," an "unpredictable and violent father," and a "grade school teacher."

The students' reactions to me as a person in authority were certainly not academic and intellectual. They were deeply tied to their personal experience. As long as the students were not aware of this, they gave me and other faculty extraordinary power that was not based upon the real situation and context, but on what happened to them long ago. Once aware, they were able to reclaim their personal power. They still reacted in the same ways, although not to the same degree. They still had some of the same feelings, but with awareness they had choice.

The most empowering interpersonal skill is the ability to look inside and gain awareness of the origins of your reactions. You do not have to understand when, how, and why you react. You only need to be aware that your here–and–now reaction *ain't* all outside yourself. That awareness puts you in the driver's seat. And further, if you are able to verbalize that your reaction comes from you, not from what the other person is doing, you differentiate your interaction.

Your initial differentiation task was to turn 180 degrees and separate what was inside you from what was going on outside of you.

(Separate Inside from Outside)

Inside		Outside
"I feel"		"it"
"I think"		"they"
"I want"		"you"
		"we"
		"one"

Next, just as you engaged in mutual inquiry and you described, listened and learned what was inside the other, the

The most empowering skill is the ability to look inside and gain awareness of the origins of your reactions.

two of you were able to separate and differentiate from each other.

Learning

(Mutual Inquiry: Separate Self from Other)

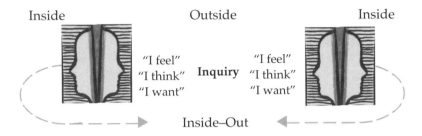

Your differentiation task now is to separate the person or situation that faces you from the historical images you bring from your past.

Learning

(Self–Inquiry: Separate Now from Then)

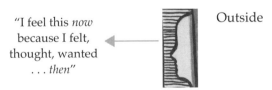

Your signal is the degree of emotional intensity you feel. When the emotional intensity is high, it's likely that you are projecting past experiences on the other, just as the students were with me.

Brad and Mary

If Brad and Mary continued their mutual inquiry, it is highly likely that both would discover how their past was affecting their here–and–now difficulty.

Brad: "Mary, I get why I've been so upset! You see, I was the oldest child in our family and had to be responsible for the other kids because both my parents worked. My youngest sister was a pain. She was able to do anything she wanted. She got away with murder. I really resented her for that. I'm afraid you've been painted with that brush."

We judge ourselves by our intentions. We judge others by their impact.

This quote by John Wallen captures our dilemma in a very few succinct words. This is the fundamental rule of the game that we normally play. Given our automatic reflexes and what comes naturally, we judge others by the impact they have on us. We judge ourselves by our intentions.

There is just one small problem with this game. That is, from the inside–out, we all *create* the impact that others have on us. To understand the impact, we need to look at ourselves, not judge others.

Acknowledging this fact blows the whole game—the rules, roles, outcomes, and the payoffs. It introduces a fundamentally different game, which is to learn about yourself *from* the impact others have on you.

To own that you create the impact others have on you is, without a doubt, the most difficult and the most important lesson to learn. In any situation, when you choose to recognize that *you* create the impact others have on you, you begin to learn and your personal power soars. When you cannot, or do not, you wind up teaching and preaching to others and remain dumb and often a victim.

The consequences of not having this awareness are great. Businesses and fortunes are lost, organizations crippled, relationships ruined and made toxic. Wars are fought. Lives are lost. And all for not making the split–second decision to turn

To own that you create the impact others have on you is, without a doubt, the most difficult and the most important lesson to learn.

from the behavior of the person outside and identify the location of and responsibility for the *impact*—inside.

Here's an illustration. I went to my health club to work out. There is one particular treadmill that I like because it is positioned in from of CNN television. It allows me to watch the news while I exercise. One day, just as I was about to climb on the treadmill, another man stepped in front of me. He didn't acknowledge me, or the fact that I arrived slightly before him. It was as though I did not exist.

The impact of his behavior was instant. My *feeling* was irritation. My *judgment* was "Who the hell does he think he is?" I *wanted* to let him know how "rude" he was. My *action* was to stand there and glare at him.

To own the impact others have on you is a solitary, existential decision. Only you can make it.

What happened next was a real lesson. He turned his head, looked surprised and said, "Oh, did I take the treadmill you wanted?" He started to get off. "I apologize. I'm blind in my left eye and didn't see you standing there."

This event was so definitive and clear that I could not duck, dodge, or weave to avoid the realization that *I created the impact he had on me*. I judged him, reacted to him, and made attributions about him. Many interactive events are often less clear, and leave us with lots of wiggle room to avoid our responsibility.

His life just improved considerably because I had to face the fact that I created the impact of his behavior on me. He wasn't the problem—I was. It works the other way around as well. *My* life would improve considerably if others would accept that responsibility for themselves.

Not long ago I was driving in Portland, an unknown city to me, and I suddenly realized that I had to cross two lanes on my left in about one city block to get on the freeway. I saw one car in my rear view mirror coming up from behind. I had to cut in front of it in order to make my turn, and I did not want to make him slow down. Since I was driving a Corvette, I accelerated out of his way.

I felt virtuous. After all, I had accomplished my task and done him a favor. My reward? A huge fist with the center finger extended.

Then I did the same thing. I made myself irritated because he misinterpreted my intention. My first impulse was to get him to change his reaction to me. Both of us could improve our lives considerably if, in that microsecond, we were to turn inside and own the impact of the other's behavior.

However, that is not how we are wired. We naturally focus outside and try to get others to own *their* stuff. We forget whose job is whose. I wish I had a buck for every time I have had someone misuse this principle by saying to another, "The impact I had on you is *your* problem, not mine!"

It is truly amazing how cleverly our out–there–outside–other–object orientation sneaks in and derails learning.

Nobody can make you own the impact they have on you. You cannot make anybody else own the impact you have on them. To own the impact others have on you is a solitary, existential decision. Only you can make it.

There will be times when every muscle, neuron and cell in your body screams out and resists that 180 degree turn to the inside. Regardless of whether you do it in the moment with the other person; or if you return the next hour, next day or much later and learn it by yourself; if you learn, you face the fact that *you* create, author, play out and sustain the impact that outside situations, events and others have on you.

This does not mean that you should let others off the hook for their behavior, or that you let others walk all over you.

It does not mean that you tolerate behavior that is uncomfortable or offends you. It also doesn't mean that you "should" or "shouldn't" be impacted as you are.

Ten thousand people, including a minister, priest, rabbi and your parents, may agree with you that your reaction is fully understandable and justified. They may unanimously agree that they would have exactly the same reaction. They may "know exactly how you feel" and tell you that "everybody has that reaction to him." All that doesn't matter.

When you explain and make excuses for the significant caretakers in your life, watch out.

It means that if someone interrupts you, that may be disruptive, but your interpretation and feelings are yours. If someone cuts in line ahead of you in traffic, that behavior may be dangerous, but your judgments and feelings are yours. If someone takes advantage of you, your interpretations, attributions and feelings are yours. If you have stage fright about an upcoming presentation, those feelings are yours.

If you intend to learn, you must accept that you create your interpretations, attributions, and feelings; they belong to you and reside inside you.

I've stressed this point for three reasons. First, to acknowledge it may be very difficult. You are called upon to transcend the undifferentiated muck and be your best. Second, this awareness opens the door to the world of self–inquiry. Finally, when you take responsibility for the impact others have on you, not only are you able to learn, you also reclaim your personal power. You are immediately transported from "done–unto" reality to the "do–unto" reality. You become less dependent, less of a victim. You are able to make choices, and are more in charge.

Become Aware of Defenses

I'm not sure why it is often difficult for us as "grown ups" to acknowledge that our past often shapes our reactions and responses to what is going on here and now, but it is. We tend to think that as adults, we *should* have put all this early stuff behind us.

"Now I'm big. Then I was little. I don't need to spend time on history."

"I had a wonderful, idyllic childhood."

"I had a painful childhood, but my parents did the best they could."

Or, as a highly stressed manager said to me while exploring some history because his health was threatened, "This is hokey."

When you think everything was "perfect," watch out. When you explain and make up excuses for the signficant caretakers in your life, watch out.

A graduate student of mine once said with admiration for her father, "He was taking care of himself" referring to an incident when he abandoned her and her little brother to fend for themselves when she was only seven!

The point, of course, is that what happened to you as a child is far less important than the meaning you gave it. From your inside–out, you created your fantasies and reality. It doesn't matter how difficult it was for your caregivers, or what great parents they were. It doesn't matter whether they did the best they could under the conditions, or whether you understand their behavior now.

What mattered was your internal experience then. What got locked into your neurological patterns was the meaning and sense you made internally way back when; even when, by all external measures, everything appeared to be going swimmingly.

With this perspective, I believe we *all* have our wounds, some greater than others. I don't believe many can escape the impact of being very, very little in a world where everybody else is very, very big. However, even if this is not true, we have all learned characteristic ways of being in the world that may have worked then, but keep us from learning now.

The more you recognize and understand how your past influenced your present, the more you can truly experience here and now.

Short Takes

To learn from within, you need to:

- notice, not try to change yourself;
- acknowledge that your past impacts the present;
- own the impact others have on you;
- understand your defenses; and
- the more you are capable of learning from within, the more you will learn from the real people who are in front of you now.

Part 3
Application Lessons

Application Lessons

These lessons give you the methods to uncover and discover here–and–now information in all kinds of settings. If the first part of the book is a guided tour through relationships and interactions, then these methods and techniques will give you the tools to be out on your own.

In a way, my job stops with these lessons—yours begins.

Before beginning, I want to emphasize three ideas that I believe will help you, just as they have me. First, I hope you will continually revisit the very fragile and illusive idea of what it means to learn. In normal life, to learn means that you'll learn procedures so that you can do things right the first time and every time.

Well, things will go "wrong." There will be times when you learn, and there will be times when you don't. There will be times when you think you do it all "right," and wind up wondering what went "wrong." So don't think that these methods will make all relationships go well. There is far too much mystery and we're far too complex to have that as an implicit goal. Just keep in mind that when your goal is to learn, *it isn't what you do or did—it's what you do **next***.

Second, while all these are methods to learn from differences—-different perspectives, different stories, different individuals—the more you use them, the more you'll discover how similar we all are. The route to similarity is through difference. Differentiation precedes integration.

Finally, since we are all "wired" in ways that block learning, the secret to becoming a skilled learner is to practice, practice, practice. . . and then practice some more.

If you are learning, it isn't what you do or did—it's what you do <u>next</u>.

In **Application Lesson 4, On Your Own**, are exercises that you can use by yourself in any setting to sharpen your awareness to look inside, face the truth of inside-out and practice differentiation. I recommend that you get in the habit of practicing these because they are common skills to learning from all the other lessons: Systems Inquiry, Mutual Inquiry and Self–Inquiry.

Application Lesson 1
HOW TO CONDUCT SYSTEMS INQUIRY

In this chapter you'll learn how to:
- ■ identify the relevant system;
- ■ discover how your system works;
- ■ observe here–and–now patterns;
- ■ use patterns to hypothesize about macro issues; and
- ■ change to learning patterns.

Bill, a former student of mine, was an internal consultant to a large organization. He asked me to conduct training to help change the organization's culture. He was skilled in our methods and theories, so he was also a member of the training staff.

During our initial planning session, he continually challenged me and my leadership of the six–person training team. Time was limited and stress was high, yet he delayed us by arguing over small points. Bill repeatedly contradicted my ideas. I listened and tried to understand why he was so "obstinate." I stated and restated my position, let him know the impact of his behavior, and expressed my frustration.

My mind raced to figure him out. "He must be really threatened. Is this because he is a former student? Is he trying to get back at me as an authority figure?"

After some discussion, we realized what was happening. We were participating in two different systems, and were unclear about which was which.

Bill was responsible for one system, *changing the organization's culture.* He brought me into his organization, but was accountable to his vice president for the results. From his framework, I worked for him. He saw his words as more than input—they were orders.

To me, we had clarified the contract, set the goals and parameters, and had entered a new system—to *design the training.* He worked for me as a member of the training staff. His input to the design was just that—input, not decisions.

The problem was that each of us operated from a different system. As a result, we had different roles and assumptions. We needed boundaries to protect each of the systems from interference by the other.

After we discovered our two systems and roles, we decided that when he spoke as the agent in charge of *changing the organizational culture,* he would sit in a specific chair. That would trigger me to hear what he said as my "boss." When he spoke as a member of the staff *designing the training*, he sat in another chair. Then it would be clear to both of us that I was in charge and would make the final decision.

Two systems, and some of the same people were involved in both. Clarification came when we set boundaries and learned. After the change, our patterns of interaction became supportive of the right system. After that, plans progressed smoothly, much to everybody's relief.

Identify the Relevant System

In order to conduct inquiry into a system, you must first identify and define it. A small, isolated interpersonal problem may relate to an interdepartmental issue. . .which may relate to company policy. . . which may relate to the federal government and its policies. . . which relate to international trade. . . which relates to food production . . . which relates to the seasons. . . which relates to the tilt of the Earth. . . and on and on. So, how do you begin?

1. Identify the Purpose

The more you practice systems thinking, the more you must revisit and identify the purpose of the organization, the team, the meeting, one section of the meeting, one contribution, one conversation, and the very words you use *now*.

In the above example, Bill and I had what appeared to both of us as an interpersonal conflict. We thought the problem was caused by the other's individual quirks, such as control and authority issues, psychic warts, motives, feelings, and the way we were raised. However, when we clarified that there were two purposes, it became clear that the problem was not interpersonal at all. It was systemic. While we squabbled, I was trying to meet one purpose, and he another. We operated from within two systems.

The important point here is to *define the purpose as specifically as possible*. For example:

System 1: Change the organizational culture.

System 2: Design and deliver the training.

2. List the Players

When you identify the system, you must also identify the people within the system. In my example with Bill, one system (design and deliver training) included me and the other staff members in the room. The other system (change the organizational culture) included Bill as agent, his vice president as sponsor, me and the training team, and many more individuals who were not in the room.

The individuals and groups identified constitute the system. They are the folks whose patterns of behavior, relationships and interactions either facilitate or hinder movement toward achieving your purpose.

These steps are among the most useful to master because they are the foundation of all the skills and methods that follow. If you can't identify the system, you can't change it.

Discover How Your System Works

All the small patterns of behavior become set over time. People in a particular system communicate with some, but ignore others. Some are in conflict over the purpose. Some are clearly in collusion over a particular issue. If you disagree with one, you'll probably have to take on the others. These consistent patterns leave people in different proximity to each other given the identified issue. The characteristics of these relationships can be shown graphically. The picture of the system is called a map.

Map the System

This method is extremely useful when you are confused about what to do when something doesn't work. It clarifies, gives direction and specific steps you can take as an individual or with others in the system.

1. Write the purpose on the top of a blank sheet of paper.
2. Place individuals in the system in relation to each other. Draw circles to represent the individuals or groups listed as the system. Use an entire page. Place the circles in relationship to you as you currently see them. The purpose of this is to uncover and discover what you believe is true.

Here's my map of the two systems described above:

If you cannot identify the system, you cannot change it.

System 1: Change the Organizational Culture

System 2: Design and Deliver Training

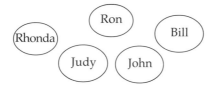

3. Graphically portray the relationships. Connect as many of the players as possible, given the above identified issue. Use the following code to graphically portray the relationships.

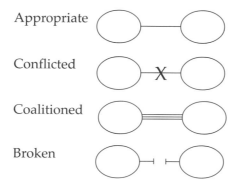

4. Identify who has the executive authority and responsibility for this system by a line under the appropriate circle. Here's an example:

System 1: Change the Organizational Culture

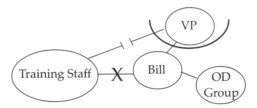

System 2: Design and Deliver Training

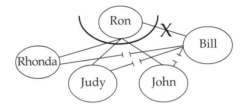

5. Follow steps 2 through 4, only this time as the system would be if it were working. Graphically portray the proximity of the participants and their relationships *as if the system worked perfectly*. For example:

System 1: Change the Organizational Culture

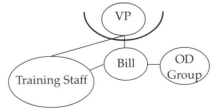

System 2: Design and Deliver Training

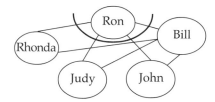

6. Develop a list of action steps you can take to go from the first to the second map. Here's an example:

    ■ Have Bill change seats when he is the "boss" and when he is a staff member.

    ■ Change System 2 to have *all* staff members talk directly to each other, not to me.

    ■ Go with Bill to meet with the VP to clarify and establish roles in System 1.

    You can map a system as an individual, which gives you clarity. However, when the real people in the system participate with you, compare maps and decide on action steps, the greater the learning, and the greater the potential for constructive change.

Observe Here—and—Now Patterns

    You can use this in any circumstance. After you develop a degree of skill, you will actually notice the patterns that you and other people create in the moment. To do this, you need your "observer."

1. Engage your observer to look for what's happening *now* inside you. What do you feel now? What do you want now? What judgments do you have now? What are you doing now?

2. Shift to your observer and suspend trying to understand what is being said and why. Simply listen to *how* it is being

said. Your observer should listen very simply and use any metaphors that, to you, capture the here–and–now pattern. Here are some questions to help your observer as he or she listens:

- What is the pattern? (For this it is useful to suspend your linear, left, figure–it–out brain and simply associate with what you hear.) Does the pattern remind you of a game? If so, what kind. A tennis match? Golf? Bridge?
- Does it remind you of a dance? What kind? A foxtrot? Tango? Waltz?
- Who talks most? Who talks least? Who talks after whom? Who interrupts whom?
- How do you characterize the tones of voice? Is one dominant, comanding, declarative, apologetic or whiny?
- How old are the voices? Young or old?
- Are the patterns or interactions congruent with the roles? For example, does the learner sound like a learner? Does the teacher sound like a teacher? Does the boss talk like a leader or a subordinate?

For example, I was once a consultant at a planning meeting held by a self–directed work team made up of four women and one man. As they developed their plans, I realized that something else was going on. Historically, it seemed as if the man was constantly in trouble with the women. Once again they argued, as in "yes. . . but; yes. . . but; yes. . . but." They made no progress and I wasn't sure why.

My observer took a look inside and said "hmmm. . . I'm irritated too." I decided to ignore what they said and, instead, listen for the pattern. I closed my eyes, tilted my head back and heard a woman's voice, immediately followed by the deeper man's voice. Then again, another woman's voice, immediately followed by the man. Woman–man, woman–man, woman–man; high–low, high–low, soprano–bass, alto–bass, soprano–bass.

He responded to *every* statement, which irritated the women. Quite naturally, because of their pattern, they addressed every statement to him so he would respond, then they would get irritated, and so on. A great example of circular causation.

Observe Non–Learning Patterns

In watching groups and teams in action, I've noticed a very interesting phenomenon. Even as people try their best to learn from each other, they automatically fall back on a few very predictable patterns that actually hide the information they need. Even when they know *how* to learn, *intend* and *want* to learn, they seem to be "hard wired" and revert to patterns that absolutely guarantee they will not and cannot learn.

Since I have learned to look for learning, I see these few patterns happen with everyone, everywhere, all the time, and in every organization. If I were a biologist, I would be tempted to say that these patterns are genetic, inherited, instinctual, and part of the way our brains are soldered to our tongues.

I have numerous tapes of groups in the process of learning how to learn from each other, and I would personally bet my professional reputation on the fact that if I play any tape at random and stop it at any point, I will observe one, if not all seven, of the following non–learning patterns.

The common attribute of these patterns is the absence of boundaries. All create undifferentiated interactions.

The common attribute of non–learning patterns is the absence of boundaries.

Pattern 1: Talking about "It"

It can be anything—a situation, event, object, another person, beliefs. . . whatever. My daughter, Sarah, and I talked about football rather than discuss how we felt about TV and football. You don't learn from your interactions when you talk only about *it* or an object and do not disclose here–and–now why you are talking about it, how you feel talking about it, and how you feel talking with the other person about it.

If you want an undifferentiated interaction with made–up stories that aren't checked out, that contain no real information and no learning, and with a high probability of leading to unnecessary disagreement and conflict, all you have to do is:

1. Pick a topic that has more than a slight emotional impact on the people involved.

2. Create a rule that people are to talk only about *it*. The *it* can be the national or organizational budget, the president, your last meeting, or an action you should take.

3. Strictly follow and enforce the meta rule: "You cannot, under any circumstances, change Rule 2 and talk about what is inside you *now*."

Pattern 2: Talking in Generalities

After all these years of observation, I am struck by how automatically we avoid a particular here–and–now event by generalizing. For example, a misinterpretation between a particular man and woman becomes a "gender issue;" or because one person is interrupted by another, "the group" doesn't function well.

I've learned to listen for certain words that give this one away. "People" often hides a discussion about you, me, or the individuals in the room. "Groups" often covers a conversation about *this* group. The use of pronouns like "they," "we," "you," and "everyone" may hide that the subject is actually "I."

For example, "Everyone complains about what is going on around here." This completely detours any potential for learning because it may hide, "I am very disatisfied with our workload."

Once you experience a live, here–and–now dialogue on something that matters to you, you'll see how hypnotic it is to speak in general terms about general topics using general vocabulary. It removes you from any potential life trying to blossom now, in the room, among and between you.

Pattern 3: Talking Hypothetically

It is very common to avoid inside–out, here–and–now conversation by talking hypothetically. I don't know how many times I've heard things like: "When I'm in a group, I . . ." while that person sits in a group. Or "If people would do this, then I could. . ." which hides "I want you to. . ."

Pattern 4: Using Questions to Hide Statements

"Haven't we made this decision before?" hides "I do not want to revisit this decision one more time." "Have we been here two hours?" probably means something like "I want to leave."

Pattern 5: Talking in the Third Person About Someone Who is Present

There are a number of fascinating ways to avoid talking directly to another person. One that comes up time and time again is talking *about* a person who is present.

Pattern 6: Talking to Anybody Except the Person Who Can Use the Information

Whenever two or three people are gathered together, there is a triangle with people who talk about individuals who are not present. This is so important that it is covered more extensively later.

Pattern 7: Speaking in the Passive Voice

"It broke" was my four–year–old daughter's favorite phrase when she dropped or damaged something. Listen randomly in most meetings and you'll wonder how "grown up" we adults really are.

Observe Learning Patterns

We'll cover learning patterns extensively in the next lesson, but for now it is sufficient to say that a learning pattern happens when:

- Two people talk directly to each other about what is inside them *now*.
- You are descriptive of the here–and–now impact you have on the other.
- You inquire.
- You make individual choices based on shared information.

Use Patterns to Hypothesize About Macro Issues

Over the years I have become convinced that small, minute–by–minute interactions are nested in and supportive of larger patterns that characterize a whole organization. How people interact in a meeting provides clues or hypotheses to the patterns in the whole organization. I have found that the very first interactions I have with a client often give me hypotheses and hunches about the whole organization that I can test as I learn more. For example:

- If our meetings constantly get interrupted, or if people are exceptionally careful not to offend—does the organization set boundaries?
- If the person speaks in non–committal and non–declarative language—is the organization clear?
- If a person can't make a decision—does the organization have difficulty making decisions?

- If a person has difficulty saying no—does the organization have difficulty holding people accountable?
- If a person is clear, declarative and no–kidding decisive to an extreme—does the organization have difficulty involving people?

Patterns simply are. And small, micro, minnie, molecular, mite– and byte–sized patterns that happen in every interaction, in every part of the organization, can give you hunches and hypotheses about the larger system–wide patterns.

Change to Learning Patterns

When Stuck

Action, not understanding, brings change. Sounds simple, doesn't it? After all, you need only to behave differently. Sometimes it is simple; often it's not.

Patterns exist for both practical and emotional reasons. Sometimes you can't know those reasons until *after* the patterns change. Therefore, if you change your patterns, you may experience a high degree of emotional resistance. For this reason it is very useful to:

- be clear about the map and your purpose for changing patterns; and
- inform everyone involved about these principles and explain why you are making the changes.

What follows is an illustrative example. Although the event took place over a decade ago, everybody involved remembers it vividly to this day. This one incident, a "lazer–diamond–cutting" intervention, left a profound and lasting effect.

As director of a graduate program with a small group of faculty, I wanted to introduce the idea of systems and systemic patterns into our graduate program. With this goal in mind, I invited Jorge Colapinto, a systems consultant, to help us with a faculty meeting. To make this a learning event for students, we decided to have them observe a faculty meeting.

There we were, a faculty of 5, conducting a meeting in front of approximately 30 or more students. The faculty sat in a circle and Jorge paced around on the outside. After the meeting started, Judy surfaced an agenda item which could be solved in a short period of time.

Patterns exist for both practical and emotional reasons.

She felt bad that she wasn't carrying her share of the workload to transport and set up video equipment. Denny, another faculty member, did it all. Judy thought it was unfair, but she "wasn't technically inclined and didn't know how to set it up." The dialogue about how Denny could teach her went on for a brief period, then came the surprise.

Jorge: (to Denny and Judy) "How soon can you teach her how to set up the equipment?"

Both Denny and Judy pulled out their calendars and tried to find a time in the coming weeks when both were available (our pattern).

Jorge: "How soon can you do it?"

They looked into the next week. At this point Denny grudgingly acknowledged that he could possibly do it sooner if he shifted some things around. . . obviously at some sacrifice to himself.

Jorge: "I said, how soon can you do it?"

And then came the moment of truth. Denny looked at Judy, stood up, and said "Come on, let's go do it now."

They walked out and left me to lead the meeting with two–fifths of the faculty gone! I was stunned, shocked and irritated; but I understood that Jorge had challenged our patterns. He did precisely what I wanted him to do. I was amused at my reaction, and the students had a great time laughing at us.

This was a dramatic way to learn a very fundamental lesson. That is, our *real* problem was not the video tape, nor Judy's feelings, but our patterns—the more Denny did, the less anybody else had to do. And we used faculty meetings to talk and talk, and plan and plan how and when we would do something rather than just do it.

All of us are caught up in patterns that we do not recognize or control, but rather, control us. Patterns are notoriously sneaky and, as was true with us, sometimes we don't even recognize them until someone behaves differently. Attempting to identify these subtle patterns is like fish trying to discover water.

If you and *your* organization is stuck in some way that you don't understand, one form of learning is simply to act differently—and be prepared to learn from the inevitable reaction. (It may help if all the folks in your system understand these principles about patterns. You may seem less weird to them if they do.)

Our real problem was not the video tape, nor Judy's feelings, but our patterns.

Detriangulate

There is one ubiquitous, non–learning pattern that ties, binds and gags every organization, group and person from learning every day and everywhere. Simply put, this pattern happens when you talk *about* another person rather than talk *to* them. It is called triangulation because it involves the relationships between three people. Here's some examples of how it works:

(A) talks to (B) about (C).

(A) asks (B) to deliver feedback to (C).

Here's a tricky one—(B) gives feedback about (A) to (C), and asks for it to be delivered to (D).

How about when (C) and (B)'s relationship is consumed with talk about (A), or about (A+D)?

Here are some practical examples you may have experienced:

- You receive collated, averaged, sanitized, summarized anonymous feedback about your performance from your colleagues through Human Resources.
- You hear from your boss that your colleagues are unhappy with you.
- You have a peer who has a friendship and considerable influence with your boss.
- Your friendly internal consultant staff member is there to "help" you, and you know the conditions of your work team will be reported to your boss.
- You walk into a meeting and everybody gets quiet, then you hear through a third party everything that your colleagues said *about* you, rather than *to* you.

There is no way misattribution, misinformation, and misinterpretation can be clarified unless individuals talk directly to each other.

Triangles simply are, have always been, and always will be. They are now and forever. They are very useful for many purposes. (Have you bought a car and the salesperson took your offer into the office to talk with the manager? Or have you used an outside consultant?)

If your goal is to learn, however, triangles are deadly. You cannot learn from anonymous feedback. There is simply no way misattribution, misinformation, and misinterpretation can be clarified unless individuals talk directly to each other.

Triangles can also make you feel crazy because the essence of non–learning triangles is often total and complete denial that people have talked about you, along with misinformation about what they have said. The silent handshake of secrecy on everybody's part is what makes the game. When this is true, *you're* not crazy. Rather the pattern of triangulation and denial is crazy–making.

If your goal is organizational pathology, I do not know of a better pattern to establish, fuel and maintain. However, if your goal is to learn, and your relationships get in the way of your quality of life, and the cost to you is excessive, then you must courageously detriangulate your relationships. To do this:

1. Identify and list specific individuals whom you have talked about, or who you think have talked about you.

2. Inform the person you have talked with about what you are going to do.

3. Go directly to each of the individuals you have listed for the purpose of learning.

Detriangulation can happen in a team with everybody present. In fact, the essence of any constructive, effective team building exercise is detriangulation. When all members of a system do this together, an amazing amount of energy is released. Triangulation is deadly. Getting straight and clean by detriangulating can be enormously energizing.

The essence of any constructive, effective team building exercise is detriangulation.

Obviously, the prospect of detriangulation may be scary. It is helpful to keep two things in mind. First, chances are extremely high that the other person has also talked about you, and also feels the pain of it. You're probably not alone. Second, there *are* steps you can take to detriangulate that will give you and others confidence. This information is included in Application Lesson 2, How to Conduct Mutual Inquiry.

Use Triangles Constructively

Enroute to detriangulation, it may be helpful to make a stopover and talk with another person. This time, however, talk in a constructive manner. Seek out a competent colleague, a friend or professional before you talk with those whom you have identified above. The task is not to discuss somebody else, but to talk *about yourself* so that you become more grounded and clear.

By doing this, you'll be more informed about your own

judgments, fears, concerns and hooks. You'll learn specific steps you can take to make this happen in Application Lesson 3, How to Conduct Self–Inquiry.

Short Takes

■ Purpose defines a system.

■ Learn to recognize non–learning and learning patterns.

■ Changing to learning patterns is the key.

Application Lesson 2
HOW TO CONDUCT MUTUAL INQUIRY

In this chapter, you'll learn how to:

- ■ agree to learn;
- ■ do the dance of mutual inquiry;
- ■ describe;
- ■ invite; and
- ■ know when to quit.

Now you know that mutual inquiry is far more than a superficial technique to get the other person to do what you want him or her to do. Rather, it means to go through the looking glass to discover and experience a different "do unto" reality. No small thing, so it will help if you:

- ■ don't take yourself too seriously;
- ■ are curious; and
- ■ give yourself and the other person considerable grace.

Agree to Learn

Where do you start? People typically approach events ready to teach, not learn. We have things to tell and sell. We want others to learn from us, but typically are far less prepared to learn from them. For that reason, it is essential that we agree to learn. It is my experience that learning will not occur if this agreement is either explicitly or implicitly absent, regardless of your skills.

There is nothing more static, predictable and boring than two teachers trying to teach each other. Nobody teaches without a learner.

Both parties must be open to learning about themselves. It's that simple. If both people mutually agree to learn about themselves, not just teach, the probability that mutual learning will take place increases exponentially.

Although I wrote the agreement below primarily to communicate what I mean by agreeing to learn, you may also find it useful:

"Our goal is to learn. This means that, to the best of our ability, we will do the following:

■ Share information and make individual choices rather than try to change the other person. Our goal is to change the relationship with information, not each other.

■ Be prepared to learn about ourselves.

■ Invite descriptive stories from each other.

■ Accept each others' stories; not as *the* truth, but as our separate, individual truths.

■ Be true to our individual stories and what is real to each of us, while being open to new information.

■ When feeling defensive, report that we are."

Do the Dance

The following describes the "dance" that takes place when two people learn. It graphically illustrates the essence of a dialogue that takes place when two parties learn about the other and about themselves.

What really happens between two people is never as clear and clean as the chart makes it appear. We talk, ramble, explain, defend, and generally fill the air with words. The

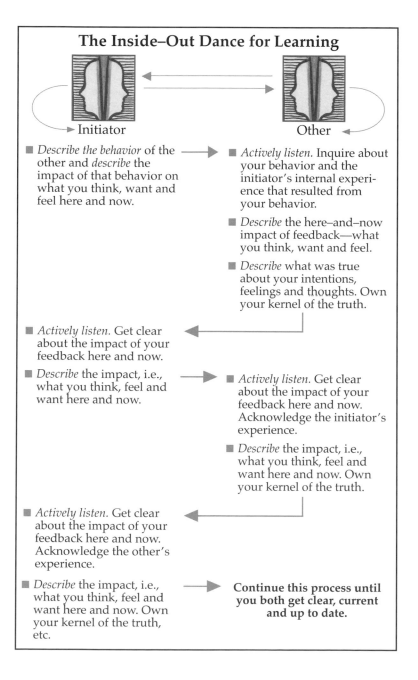

The Inside–Out Dance for Learning

Initiator

- *Describe the behavior* of the other and *describe* the impact of that behavior on what you think, want and feel here and now.

- *Actively listen.* Get clear about the impact of your feedback here and now.

- *Describe* the impact, i.e., what you think, feel and want here and now.

- *Actively listen.* Get clear about the impact of your feedback here and now. Acknowledge the other's experience.

- *Describe* the impact, i.e., what you think, feel and want here and now. Own your kernel of the truth, etc.

Other

- *Actively listen.* Inquire about your behavior and the initiator's internal experience that resulted from your behavior.

- *Describe* the here–and–now impact of feedback—what you think, want and feel.

- *Describe* what was true about your intentions, feelings and thoughts. Own your kernel of the truth.

- *Actively listen.* Get clear about the impact of your feedback here and now. Acknowledge the initiator's experience.

- *Describe* the impact, i.e., what you think, feel and want here and now. Own your kernel of the truth.

Continue this process until you both get clear, current and up to date.

process can appear to be terribly complex. We are especially vulnerable to being blown off course when we have intense feelings.

When you are confused, simplify. To do your part of the dance and tack back on course, you need to ask yourself only two questions:

1. Am I being descriptive?

2. Am I inviting the other to be descriptive?

Describe

Being descriptive is a learned, disciplined choice organized by the intention to learn.

The idea is simple. "I like orange juice" is descriptive. "I'm from Colorado" is descriptive. "I live in Seattle now" is descriptive. No arguments, right?

Now, look a little closer. "I was bored watching yesterday's baseball game" is also descriptive. "I got up early this morning and feel impatient because I haven't written much." Descriptive facts. No arguments, right?

Brad and Mary

Now look at the same idea even more closely, using a sentence from Brad and Mary's dialogue (see Underlying Dynamic, on page 70):

Brad: (a little nervous) "Mary, I'm really getting tired of being the person who carts all our stuff around and makes sure everything is o.k. I want some help." Still descriptive fact.

Now look at this same idea, but even closer and in the present moment, here and now:

Mary: "I'm stunned and surprised. I have been thinking you *liked* doing that stuff!" Still descriptive fact, no arguments.

Mutual inquiry with another person is the pursuit of that simple idea. If the two of you can establish descriptive dialogue, you share and understand facts that are unarguable.

116

Now look out, because it is far trickier to be both descriptive and to hear description because the information isn't about orange juice, where you grew up, or baseball. It is information about the impact the two of you have on each other.

Show me a non–learning, undifferentiated interaction, and I'll show you a conversation with no description, or description that wasn't interpreted as descriptive.

When mutual inquiry goes wrong, think description. There are two basic rules to follow.

First, come "home" to what you can describe; that is, what was and is real inside of you. To simplify, search for your internal reality in three places:

1. What you *thought* and are *thinking* (attributions, judgments, beliefs).

   For example, Brad's thought was "I'm the person who carts this stuff around. . ." Mary's thought was "I've been thinking you *liked* doing this stuff. . ."

2. What you *felt* and are *feeling* (mad, sad, glad, scared and all the more precise descriptions).

   For example, Brad's felt nervous (sad) and frustrated (mad), neither of which he reported directly. Mary felt "stunned and surprised."

3. What you *wanted* and what you *want* (intentions, desires, motives).

   For example, Brad's initial desire was for "help."

Second, keep in mind that you can only describe what you can observe about the other. You can only see his or her *behavior*, what he or she is, does or has done. Your judgments, inferences, and attributions are created by you—inside of you—for your reasons. They say more about you than the other person.

Brad can observe that Mary does not help get the necessary equipment and materials to the training. He has *not* observed that she is "self–serving," a "dilettante," or a "user."

Mary can observe that Brad looked away, did not smile, and did not say good morning. She has *not* observed that he is a "grump." That is her judgment.

Be Aware of Your Choices

As I've said, being descriptive does not come naturally. First, you have to go directly against your automatic, out–there, outside other focus, turn around 180 degrees and describe yourself. Second, you need to go against what comes naturally and separate your inside thoughts from the other's behavior; what he or she is doing and did from the attributions and meaning you gave to the behavior. Not easy.

Only you can choose to be descriptive about yourself.

Others cannot command, demand, or require it.

Being descriptive is a learned, disciplined choice that is organized around one single intention—to *learn*. The longer you live with this awareness, the more you will recognize the choices that you and others routinely make enroute to mutual learning.

The fundamental behavior to look for is how much you and others describe your internal states—in routine conversations as well as in difficult, thorny interactions. With this basic premise, you can take any interaction and place it in one of four categories. The first two (hide and react) come naturally.

Category 1: Hide

I do not intend to make this a pejorative concept—I simply mean the degree to which internal, here–and–now processes are public, visible and present in a conversation. We hide in ritual conversations: "Good morning, how are you?" "Fine." We hide when we ask questions: "Do you think....?" We hide in most conversations and very appropriately so. There is absolutely nothing wrong with this choice. It is sometimes appropriate and essential. The problem comes when you want to learn.

This is a problem because, in my judgment, we hide when it's not our intention. We have an incredible repertoire of behaviors that keep us hidden. For example, we ask questions to hide what we want. We change the subject when we're hurt or angry. We talk about others or events so the focus is not on us. We use "you" language. As we get more sophisticated, we even use "I" language to hide so we can look like we're disclosing and describing when we're not.

I am convinced that this is the fundamental dilemma that we all face when we want to learn. These habitual ways of being have become so automatic that we don't recognize that we make a choice to hide. Thus, we fool not only others, but ourselves as well.

Category 2: React

This also comes very naturally—more naturally to some than others. Our emotions and feelings are basically reactions to external and internal stimuli. In interactions it shows up when we communicate through *expression* of our feelings, not *description* of them.

When you react, your focus is outside on the other, the object or event. When you react negatively, your desire is for others or the situation to change. I believe that what most folks call being open and honest is actually being reactive. I wish I had a dollar for every person who thinks he or she has learned these ideas and then uses them as an excuse to be reactive.

Category 3: Describe–but–Hide

This category is truly interesting to me having spent my professional life training people in these skills. It takes place when people are exposed to interpersonal communication skills, groups, or teaming theory and learn inside–out communications.

They use the knowledge to stay in the "done unto" reality and focus on the other object. This trained disability is so pervasive that I consider it at the epidemic level—which correctly gives my chosen profession a bad name.

Essentially, when you describe–but–hide, you use the right techniques, like "I" messages to make the *appearance* of being descriptive, while you truly hide and/or react. It looks like description, but leaves both parties dumber and deeper in the "done unto" reality after the interaction than before it started. As mentioned in the introduction, this is the way you can fool yourself.

Brad and Mary

Brad: "Mary, I'm really getting tired of being the person who carts all our stuff around and makes sure everything is o.k. I want some help."

Mary: "*I* can't believe that you are saying that to me. How can you think that *I'm* not doing my part? *I* work every bit as hard around here as you do."

Beware and be wary. None of us is immune. The "look alike" can penetrate, sneak in and take over almost any interaction very easily. These fakes come camouflaged in many different forms but you can use the following criteria to identify them.

- The focus is outside on the other even though "I" and other more sophisticated psychobabble is used.
- There is no intent to learn.

Category 4: Describe

The goal is clarity. The reality is inside–out. The responsibility is shared. Enough said.

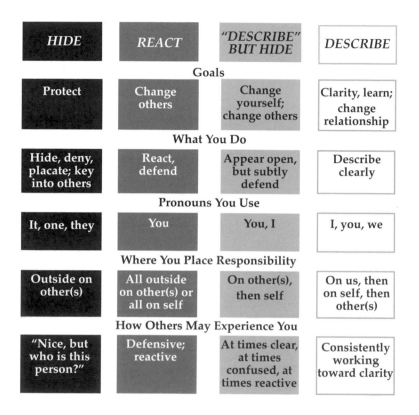

HIDE	REACT	"DESCRIBE" BUT HIDE	DESCRIBE
Goals			
Protect	Change others	Change yourself; change others	Clarity, learn; change relationship
What You Do			
Hide, deny, placate; key into others	React, defend	Appear open, but subtly defend	Describe clearly
Pronouns You Use			
It, one, they	You	You, I	I, you, we
Where You Place Responsibility			
Outside on other(s)	All outside on other(s) or all on self	On other(s), then self	On us, then on self, then other(s)
How Others May Experience You			
"Nice, but who is this person?"	Defensive; reactive	At times clear, at times confused, at times reactive	Consistently working toward clarity

Avoid the "Get the Other to Describe" Trap

Consciously or by default, most mutual inquiry conversations start with a mix of "hide," "react" and "describe–but–really hide." What happens *next* makes all the difference.

When neither you nor the other person is being descriptive, normally the wrong person begins to do the wrong persons's work. Person A tries to get Person B to be descriptive, while not being descriptive himself or herself. Person B tries to get Person A to be descriptive, while not also being descriptive. Quite literally, if I've seen it once, I've seen it a thousand times.

Brad and Mary

Brad: (defensive about Mary's defensiveness) "Mary, what's going on? What are you feeling!?"

Mary: (in response) "Brad, why are you being so defensive!?"

---

*What You Describe**

Wants are your desires, intentions and wishes for yourself, others and your relationships.

Goals	Desires	Drives
Motives	Intentions	Needs
Wishes	Objectives	Interests
Values		

Thoughts are the meanings you make out of internal and external stimuli. They include:

Interpretations	Beliefs	Expectations
Opinions	Conclusions	Objections
Requirements	Impressions	Judgments
Reasons	Analysis	Possibilities
Assumptions	Values	Attitudes
Explanations	Risks	Ideas
Hunches	Principles	Guesses
Benefits	Consequences	Predictions

Feelings are spontaneous emotional responses to your sense data and thoughts. Here is a partial list of common feelings:

Pleased	Disappointed	Confident
Frustrated	Excited	Bored
Satisfied	Proud	Angry
Comfortable	Uneasy	Happy
Hesitant	Surprised	Cautious
Eager	Disinterested	Irritated
Fascinated	Anxious	

---

*Adapted from Miller, et. al, 1988.

Most of the information to this point was designed to get you to this moment of truth: *Only you can choose to be descriptive about yourself. Others cannot command, demand, or require it. You cannot command, demand, or require another to be descriptive. This decision is, and will remain, your individual choice.*

If you intend to learn you will have to catch yourself in the act.

As for the other person, the best you can do is *invite* him or her to describe. You do this by being descriptive and listening actively to uncover the other's inside–out reality.

Brad: "Mary, your comment stops me in my tracks. It is hard to hear. I'm feeling defensive. Do you think that I am accusing you of not working enough?"

Invite

You invite another person to be descriptive by doing it yourself first. Typically, if you lead, others will follow; if you risk, others will risk; and if you trust, others will also trust.

You also invite another person to describe when you actively listen to them.

Listen and Inquire

At times, your side of mutual inquiry means stuffing your agenda to be understood in order to truly "get" the other person's story. While you want the other to understand you, often the best route is to understand the other. As you gain understanding (and true information), your story may change.

It is difficult and dangerous to actively listen because as you learn, your internal stories *will* be influenced and changed. Also, it is one thing to listen to someone who has a problem; it is quite another thing to listen when *you* are the problem.

Nothing changes until one person leans in to listen.

Brad and Mary

Let's go back to Brad and Mary to get an idea of how listening works. I'll abbreviate a tough scenario by filling in homeostatic, non–learning patterns with words that accurately portray undifferentiated, non–descriptive, non–learning patterns. The words are "blah, blah, blah."

Brad: "Mary, I'm really getting tired of being the person who carts all our stuff around and makes sure everything is o.k. I want some help."

Mary: "I can't believe you are saying that to me. How can you think that I'm not doing my part? I work hard around here! So *this* is why you've been so grumpy."

Brad: "I didn't say you don't work hard. You don't help us plan and get organized though. I can't count on you to even know where our next gig is."

Mary: "Where our next gig is! Don't you know how much time I put in on thinking about the design and how we're going to get the message across? What's important anyway?" (*Blah, blah, blah.*)

Ever been there? Done that? Without description, this conversation between Brad and Mary goes nowhere. No learning takes place. The interaction is undifferentiated and non–descriptive. I could fill five or ten more pages and the blah, blah pattern would be the same. Some points:

- Both are outside, reacting to the outside–other.
- The original problem is lost (the way they are communicating is the problem).
- Nothing changes until one person leans in to listen and invites the other to describe.

Mary: "Hey, Brad. This is going nowhere. I feel defensive, and want to stop what I'm doing and understand better. If

I heard you right, you're really getting tired of doing all the up–front preparation work. And you're upset that I'm not helping more."

Brad: "Yeh, I need you to pick up some of it. I *am* sick of doing it all myself." (Blah, blah, blah.)

Brad still sees his problem as outside himself. The blah–blah pattern continues.

Mary: (resisting the blah, blah, blah pattern and listening): "I'm getting it. Because you've been doing it, you resent that I'm not doing my fair share. Now I understand what's been going on with you lately. To tell you the truth, I've recently begun to feel a little uncomfortable that you're doing all that too."

Brad: (softening) "Well, it's not only the preparation work. To be honest I want to do more of the up–front stuff. We've gotten locked into roles and being the sherpa guide just no longer packs it for me. You look puzzled. Are you?"

Now there is movement, description, learning and differentiation. The shift in pattern was because Mary listened to understand Brad's internal reality. She suspended her need to be understood, which also gave her a space to bring up her own inside story.

Mary: "No, not puzzled; but I want you to know that recently I've found it hard to work with you too. When you walk around with your head down and don't talk to me about what's going on, I get paranoid and pull away."

Brad: "Yeah. I can see that. I want us to agree not to let this stuff simmer for so long."

Principles

From the outside–in, we often listen for and hear what is in our head; what we expect and want to hear; what will support our judgments of the other or support our perspective. Instead, listen for what the other person feels, thinks and wants:

- here and now; with you, as you listen;
- toward and about you and the topic being discussed; and
- toward and about the other's Self.

Here are some listen–and–inquire skills:

Paraphrase

To make sure you have heard and understand, repeat back to the other what she or he is saying about:

- the topic;
- his or her internal experience of the topic (thoughts, feelings and wants);
- his or her thoughts, feelings and wants towards you; and
- his or her thoughts, feelings and wants about himself or herself.

Mary: "I'm getting it. Because you've been doing it, you resent that I'm not doing my fair share. Am I right?"

Check Perceptions

Check out any inferences, attributions you have about what the talker feels, thinks or wants here and now.

Brad: "You look puzzled. Are you?"

Be Curious

Mary: "Is there more you want to tell me about that?"

Be Empathic

When you are empathic, the other person knows that you understand how he or she feels. You accept the other's virtual reality as true for him or her.

Mary: "I'm getting it—you resent that I'm not doing my fair share. Am I right?"

Learning to listen, not as a helper, but as a genuine human who seeks to learn from another is a highly sophisticated skill.

126

Help the Speaker Get Specific and Descriptive

Actively help the other person be specific and descriptive about his or her internal state and, if relevant, about your behavior that triggered it.

Demonstrate Respect

Communicate that the other person has a right to his or her internal experience. Yours may be different, but you accept the other's reality as you want yours accepted.

Be Genuine

The other person knows that you are a genuine and open human being, not a mechanical automaton practicing lessons learned in a workshop. Skill and technique take a distant back seat to being genuine.

Use Immediacy

Bring your immediate experience into the discussion to clarify what is going on here and now. Use your observer to help you first be aware of your here–and–now state, which you then share with the other person.

Summary Guidelines

- Communicate respect. Accept the other's internal experience as *his or her* truth, but not necessarily *the* truth.
- Suspend your experience (feelings, thoughts and wants), but track what is going on inside you.
- Place yourself in the other's shoes. Think what it would be like for you to say these things.
- Be congruent, open and genuine.
- Don't tell your story until you understand the other person's side (to his or her satisfaction.)

- Don't give unsolicited advice or communicate any "shoulds" or "oughta's."
- Don't take responsibility for the other's internal reality.
- Don't negate in any way the other's feelings, thoughts or desires.

Learning to listen, not as a helper, counselor or therapist, but as a genuine human who seeks to learn from another human being is a highly sophisticated skill that we never learn. There will always be times when you do not or cannot listen. Even at those times, you'll find it helpful to know that you are not listening.

Know When to Quit

There are times when you and the other person simply cannot learn from each other. It is important to know when to give up, perhaps try again later, or to give up on the relationship.

Your responsibility is to describe and invite. It is all you can do.

While you do your part, notice what keeps coming back. If, after several attempts, the other person continues to respond with "you" and other non–learning, outside–object language, reschedule and try again later. If that doesn't work and the relationship is important to you, get a third party to help. If that also fails, and you're confident that you have done your job well, change your job. Quit trying to learn in this particular relationship and start being strategic.

Short Takes

- You can only do what you can do. You cannot command, demand, or coerce another to learn.
- Learn to recognize the fundamental differences in outside–in and inside–out language.

- Take responsibility for your part; be descriptive and listen actively.
- Try to see the world through the other's eyes. (Think of it this way—if you had been on the other side of you and your behavior, you might have acted even dumber than you judge him or her to be!)
- Know when to quit.

Application Lesson 3
HOW TO CONDUCT SELF–INQUIRY

In this chapter, you'll learn how to:

- ■ use intensity as a cue;
- ■ use a friend or colleague wisely;
- ■ recognize when you're hooked;
- ■ help when two others are hooked; and
- ■ learn from a familiar pattern.

You create the impact that others have on you. To understand another's impact on you, look at yourself.

Use Intensity as a Cue

The more intense and the louder the impact, the more you can count on your reaction as a cue that all is not as it seems on the surface. Your emotional intensity is a loud signal that what is in front of you has triggered something much deeper. The more intense the reaction, the deeper and more central the issue is to you.

When the impact of a situation is very intense, the relevant information is inside you, not in the other or in the here–and–now situation. You'll be able to learn and claim your personal power, not from focusing on the other, but from connecting the dots between the current situation and your past. Even if you cannot connect all the dots, at least you are focused in the right direction.

Use a Friend or Colleague Wisely

Using a colleague wisely means turning from doing what comes naturally. When we allow our outside–other orientation to run its natural course, we turn to a colleague and talk about "it," "them," "him" or "her." We gossip, triangulate, talk about the other, and judge others based upon their impact.

Not only do we not learn, we perpetuate our helplessness.

Using a colleague wisely means to trace out the impact the other (or situation) has inside you. It means using him or her to shine the light in the right direction. It means engaging with someone who will help you become more centered. It means choosing someone who will help you get more differentiated and more in charge. *In short, it means having a trusted colleague who will help you explore yourself, not talk about the other.*

If you intend to learn, you must accept that you create your interpretations.

Recognize When You're Hooked

You know the feeling. You're going along fine then something happens, someone says something or looks the wrong way. The emotional intensity erupts inside you. Maybe there is someone who really "gets under your skin," even though he or she doesn't appear to do it intentionally. There's "just something about him or her" and it is hard to ignore the feelings. It's even harder to talk about them because you don't understand their cause. Or, maybe you *hate* meetings, or you're scared to death to make a presentation, or you are scared to give an employee some well–deserved negative feedback, or you: _____
_____ (fill in the blank).

Chances are you're "hooked." You are reactive. The intensity of your response has less to do with the situation or person in front of you than with events or persons from your past.

This is an ideal time to talk with a trusted colleague who understands the inside–out game, the importance of owning the impact, and who can listen well.

The instructions that follow are intended to help you when spontaneous events occur and you are surprised by your reaction. They can be accomplished in a matter of minutes, or take much longer; it depends on how close to the surface the cause of your reaction lies, the quality of your relationship with the listener, and the listener's skill. Sometimes it is enough know that your reaction has little to do with the here–and–now context, that it comes from the past. In any event, your goal is to own the impact. If you can discuss the situation with someone you trust, you will be less reactive, more differentiated, better able to engage with and learn from the *real* situation or person.

To own the impact others have on you is a solitary, existential decision. Only you can make it.

1. Meet with a Colleage and Reach an Agreement

Your colleague's job is to listen actively. It is your job to talk, not about the other, but about yourself.

2. Respond to Inquiry

The listener's goal is to help you understand why the incident or person hooked you. Your goal is to be more differentiated so you can make a more informed choice about what to do.

The questions below are organized to help you progressively separate a) your inside from the outside; b) yourself from the other; and c) what is going on now from your past. They are not intended to be inclusive, restrictive or required.

■ What does the other person *do* that hooks you?

Separate Your Inside from the Outside

Inside		Outside
"I feel"		"it"
"I think"		"they"
"I want"		"you"
		"we"
		"one"

- When he/she does that behavior, what do you:
  Feel toward him/her? Feel toward yourself?
  Want from the other? Want for yourself?
  Attribute to the other? Attribute to yourself?
- What do you say in response?

Separate Your Self from the Other

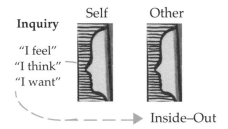

- How descriptive is it? How does it hide what you think, feel and want?
- Have you seriously listened and inquired about what the other person feels, thinks and wants?
- Does the person remind you of someone?

Separate Your Projections from the Other

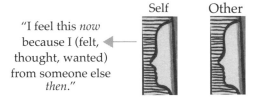

- Are your feelings toward the other familiar?
- Toward whom have you had those feelings before?
- How old do you feel when you react to the other?

Separate Your Now From Your Past

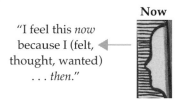

Now

"I feel this *now* because I (felt, thought, wanted) . . . *then.*"

- How is this experience similar to life as a child?
- What role do you take? Is this a familiar role?
- When is the earliest time you can remember responding as you do?

3. Check Inside

You end this exercise at any time when you have enough perspective to return to the situation or person and learn.

Call Upon a Third Party

There may be times when you and someone else need help from a third party, or you are called in to help two others who are having difficulty. This suggested procedure is for relationships where the two parties are so blinded by their accumulated "hooks" that they can't listen, describe, or give and receive information.

The goal is for both parties to get as clear as possible and own the impact the other has on them *before* they engage in mutual inquiry. When the two finally do talk directly with each other, both have searched inside to own the impact, and both know that the other has also.

Under these conditions, the probability of reaching a successful conclusion and being able to learn from each other is extremely high.

1. Agree to Learn

Once again, the agreement to learn by both parties is essential (see page 114).

2. Select a Colleague as a Third Party

Each person may select his or her own colleague, or both may select the same one. The primary criterion is whether the colleague has the skills to listen actively and lead the talkers back to themselves.

3. Prepare

Before meeting with the third party colleague, each person should:

- Write three positive and three negative adjectives about the Other.
- Select the most emotionally powerful adjective. This adjective may be either positive or negative.
- Write a description of the other's behavior that elicits this judgment or adjective.

4. Engage With the Colleague

Reach an agreement about the goal, that is to help each person get clear about the other person's impact so the parties can engage in mutual inquiry. Remember, if the talkers speak about themselves, they are doing it "right." If they talk about each other, they are doing it "wrong."

Share the adjectives. Trace out why the adjectives were selected. Below are some questions to help you get started. They are not intended to be directive or inclusive.

- Can you remember a time when you were called that adjective?
- How would you feel about yourself if you were called that?

■ When is the earliest time you can remember using that adjective? Toward whom?

■ Does this person or situation remind you of anyone or anything from your background?

5. Participate in Mutual Inquiry

After both parties have gained some clarity about why they are "hooked," or at least are aware that all of their intensity is not about the other, they are equipped to meet face to face and engage in mutual inquiry—only now they will:

■ shine the light in the right direction;

■ know something about the source of their emotional intensity;

■ understand that they have judged each other based on impact, and judged themselves based on their intentions; and

■ know that the other knows.

The probability of learning and creating a more functional relationship is now extremely high.

Learn from Familiar Patterns

There is no substitute for finding yourself in the same difficult situation over and over again, with different people, and under different circumstances and have the realization dawn: *When this happens, who's always here?* One might get the idea that "I'm the independent variable that creates and replicates this pattern over and over.

Often these consistent, repetitive patterns of behavior (that don't work for you now) worked when you were younger. The choices you made then were very functional. Problem is— today ain't then.

This is a process of using a third party to help you get current, up to date and make different choices. Engage with a colleague and answer these questions.

- Name some other times that you remember finding yourself in this pattern?
- When is the earliest time you can remember?
- What is the impact of this pattern on you? How do you feel about yourself?
- When is the earliest time you remember feeling this way?

Short Takes

- The more intense, the more your reaction says about you.
- Effective coaching helps you understand yourself.
- The clearer you are about you and your reactions, the more you will be able to learn from others.

Application Lesson 4
ON YOUR OWN

Remind Yourself: Look Inside

Purpose

   To have a conscious physical act that triggers your awareness to be present, to look inside, and check in with what is going on with you here and now.

When to Use

   This can be used at any time, whether alone or with others as a cue to shift your outside focus to the inside. It is especially useful when an interaction or meeting is not going well and you want to make different choices about what you are doing.

Method

   Routinely press your thumb and forefingers on one hand together when you focus inside. After a period of time you will be able to use this conscious voluntary act to stop your outside focus, turn around, look inside and be present.

"Faceless" Exercise:*
The Truth of Inside–Out

Purpose

   To dramatically punctuate two truths. First, you always interact from the inside–out. Second, you have some of the greatest difficulty seeing what is most obvious.

*Adapted from Harding, 1972.

When to Use

Do this exercise whenever you want to truly have the experience of looking at the world from the inside–out. This exercise takes focused concentration; therefore, it is best used alone or with others when there is the space to reflect and experience it fully.

Method

Read the following instructions in their entirety and then slowly carry them out, allowing the importance of the perspective to settle in.

Sitting in a relaxed position slowly allow your gaze to progress from your legs, your hands, up to your stomach, up your arms, up to your shoulders until they disappear.

Experience the hole, the portal, the window out of which you are looking. Spend a timed minute allowing your vision to focus on the "hole" and what it contains. Check out its boundaries. Look at your two fuzzy noses, the rims of your glasses if you are wearing them.

Notice that you have no face. Acknowledge that you never have a face because even when you look in a mirror, you do so with no face. You have never seen your face.

When you interact with another person, you swap faces.

Then close your eyes and spend a minute focusing behind your "portal." This is the area of the activity, the meaning making, the story writing.

Differenting What's Inside

Purpose

To practice making critical learning distinctions, first separate what is inside you from what is outside. And once inside, separate what you think from what you feel, from what you want. Practiced over time, this exercise will enable you to interact from the inside–out.

When to Use

This exercise can be used at any time when alone, or with someone, in any setting and should be practiced often. It is very useful when you find yourself impacted emotionally and organized outside on external events, situations or people.

Method

Press your thumb and forefingers together, turn around and identify what is going on inside (see page 139).

1. What are you thinking? About the other person, event or situation? What are you thinking about and toward your-self? This includes such activities as judgments, attributions, inferences.

2. What do you feel?

   Avoid the many traps we use to avoid identifying what we feel—like, "I feel that___," or "I feel like___" that are really thoughts.

3. What do you want? If you can only come up with what you don't want, change that into what you *do* want.

As you practice this exercise, you'll probably find one activity more difficult to contact than the others. For example, some people have easy access to their feelings, but cannot identify what they want. Others can identify what they want, but have difficulty naming what they feel. Many of us easily contact what we *don't* want or like, but have a great deal of difficulty with what we *do* want.

(I personally believe this latter is the most important because being aware of what you want directs you to a goal, and this, in turn, organizes your behavior and what you think and feel.)

Parting Words

We started this book learning from our different perspectives. I assumed that you were deciding whether to read further while I was driven to write it.

Now that you're reading this, I can safely assume that we've both completed our respective journeys.

I wonder what you walk away with. Has reading the book:

- increased your awareness?
- helped you label some of what has always been in front of you?
- aided your understanding?
- challenged you to learn from your relationships?

Of course I hope that it has.

Writing the book has had a profound effect on me. I understand more clearly than before. I know what I need to do to learn. I comprehend much better than before why learning from others is so difficult for all of us—we are neurologically wired, developmentally socialized and languaged into automatic, reflexive ways of thinking *outside* that blind us to our awareness and choice *inside.*

I am more understanding, accepting and forgiving of myself and others.

I hope some of the same is true for you because, let's face it, given the incredible challenges we face today, we've just got to do a better job of telling and listening to each other's here–and–now stories. And none of us can do it alone.

References, Influences and Resources

References

Friedman, Edwin. *From Generation to Generation.* Guilford Press, 1985.

Harding, D.E., *On Having No Head.* Perennial Library, Harper & Row, 1972.

McLagan and Nel. *The Age of Participation.* Berrett–Koehler, 1995.

Miller, Sherod; Wackman, Daniel; Nunnaly, Elam. *Connecting With Self and Others.* Interpersonal Communications Programs, 1988.

Vaill, Peter. *Learning As A Way of Being.* Jossey–Bass, 1996.

Influences

This section refers you to selected references listed under critical themes from the book.

Here and Now

This is one of the most difficult concepts to teach, to learn, and definitely to live. My favorite author is Alan W. Watts. A good example of his writing on this topic is *The Wisdom of Insecurity.* Vintage Book, 1951.

Practicing meditation is helpful.

Kabat–Zinn, Jon. *Wherever You Go There You Are.* Hyperion, 1995.

Boorstein, Sylvia, *Don't Just Do Something, Sit There.* Harper, San Francisco, 1996.

Existential Responsibility

If you read only one book about existential responsibility, read Victor Frankl's *Man's Search for Meaning*. Mass Market Paperbacks, Revised and Updated. 1998.

Kierkegaard, Soren. Heavy, serious reading, but very worthwhile. An example is *Purity of Heart*. Harper Row, 1938.

Self–Observation

Deikman, Arthur. *The Observing Self.* Beacon Press, 1982.

Self–observation is central to spiritual traditions. An example of this "mindfulness" can be found in Jack Kornfield, *A Path With Heart*, Bantam–Doubleday–Dell, 1993.

Human Systems Thinking

The person who is most often given credit for shaping our thoughts is Ludwig von Bertalanffy. *General Systems Theory.* Braziller, 1969. A very readable biography of him and his ideas is by Mark Davidson, *Uncommon Sense,* Tarcher, 1983.

In my view, family therapists lead in bringing systems ideas down to the very practical level. For an excellent historical overview that set the background for many of the concepts in this book, I recommend Michael Kerr's "Family Systems Theory and Therapy," Chapter 7 in *Handbook of Family Therapy,* Gurman and Kniskern, eds. Brunner / Mazel, 1981.

The systems ideas in the book are primarily derived from Salvador Minuchin and Structural Family Therapy. For an overview, I recommend just the first few chapters of *Familes and Family Therapy.* Harvard Press, 1974.

While being trained in structural family therapy, I struggled with how to bring the systems ideas into my educational and consultative practice. This resulted in two articles. "Structural Family Therapy and Consultative Practice: A Paradigm Shift for O.D." *Consultation: An International Journal.* Vol. 4.

Number 2. Summer, 1985 and "Structural Family Therapy and Consultative Practice." *Ibid.* Vol. 4. Number 3. Fall, 1985.

Organizational Learning

For an excellent historical background, I highly recommend Art Kleiner's *The Age of Heretics.* Bantam Doubleday Dell, 1996.

Argyris, C., and Schon, D. *Organizational Learning: A Theory of Action Perspective.* Addison–Wesley, 1978. This is important background for understanding learning in organizations. Of course today's classic is Peter Senge's *The Fifth Discipline,* Doubleday/Currency, 1990.

I present my perspective on the underlying dynamics of team learning in Short, R., *A Special Kind of Leadership: The Key to Learning Organizations.* Learning In Action, 1991.

Resources

A reference containing exercises and application ideas for learning organizations in general is Senge, P., Kleiner, A., Roberts, C., Ross, R., and Smith, B. *The Fifth Discipline Fieldbook: Strategies and Tools for Building A Learning Organization.* Doubleday-Currency, 1994.

The following are resources specifically derived from the ideas in this book. More information can be obtained from *Learning in Action Technologies, Inc.,* (206) 464–4271.

- *A Map: Learning Cultures and You.* 1995. This is a 35–page booklet that contrasts the assumptions of the dominant technical culture with those of the learning culture. It is designed to help people understand the important differences between learning techniques to manipulate outside objects and learning from others.

- A self–scored instrument and leader's guide that provides measures of Hide, React, Describe and Systems

Aware for teams to learn from their interactions. *Progress Assessment.* 1994.

■ For the purpose of identifying an individual's skill in learning, Dr. Dave Erb has created *Selection As A Learning Event.* 1994. The kit includes written instructions and a video tape of 13 scenarios of people talking directly to the user whose task is to turn inside and describe the impact. This can be used for training as well as selection purposes.

■ The *Self–Awareness Guide* distills the essential ideas in this book into a step–by–step, easy–to–read format. It provides the steps, principles, traps and self–awareness ratings for inside–out learning in a highly condensed form. The booklet can be used as a simplified guide, as well as a reminder of the cardinal skills and principles necessary to learn from relationships.

■ *Learning from Disagreement and Conflict* is a one–day, in–house seminar designed for organizations and teams. The design includes basic theory, practice, feedback and self–assessment in Turning Inside, Describing What's Inside, Inviting Descriptions and Conducting Mutual Inquiry.

Glossary of Terms

Attribution

The automatic, reflexive tendency to ascribe thoughts, motives, judgments and feelings to others. When we make attributions, we essentially are living "in the other's head, not our own." To get back in our own head requires looking inside and describing our thoughts, motives and feelings that drive the attributions.

Boundaries

A boundary establishes and differentiates one system from another. Its function is to define the rules of who is in, who is out, what is talked about with whom, and to protect one sub-system from interference from another.

Dialogue

Dialogue is a direct, free-flow of information between at least two people that results in discoveries and mutual learning.

Differentiation

The capacity to be true to oneself while simultaneously being in relationship and open to others.

Differentiated Interactions

The hallmark of a differentiated interaction is when individuals speak for themselves, describing and owning their internal states. The result is clarity. All parties in the interaction know, or can ask for and receive, the motives, feelings and thoughts of others.

Experience

As used in this book, experience is the internal here–and–now meanings that you ascribe to external events and others. Your here–and–now experience is an internal state, being continuously created by you, that consists of your thoughts, feelings and wants. Your experience is not created by what others do to you, but what you do internally with what others do.

Feelings

Feelings are the spontaneous emotional responses to both internal and external stimulation. They include mad, sad, glad and scared, and the refinements of these.

Human System

The individuals and relationships that are constituted to meet a given purpose.

Interactions

The here–and–now process of individuals communicating, using both verbal and nonverbal cues.

Learning

As used in this book, learning is increasing one's awareness about one's internal state, the internal state of others and making an *informed* choice about what to do.

Learning Culture

A learning culture is a collective phenomenon that emerges from expectations that everybody will be appropriately open about inferences, judgments, attributions, desires and feelings. You'll know you are in a learning culture when you feel free to be yourself and are expected to routinely bring what is going on inside you to the table. Cheating in a learning culture means to have information and not share it.

Learning Patterns

As used in this book, a learning pattern is the "Dance of Mutual Inquiry" that clarifies misunderstandings between two people. It results in clarity. It leads to a differentiated interaction.

Learning Relationship

In a learning relationship you mutually expect each other to be open about inferences, judgments, attributions, desires and feelings when appropriate. The relationship is marked by mutual respect and trust. Conflict and disagreement are openly dealt with in a timely fashion. *Note:* A learning relationship is not necessarily a friendship, as you can be friends and not be open.

Mutual Inquiry

A pattern of direct, open interaction between two parties that brings clarity about their internal states. It is the "dance" that inevitably takes place when two people become clear about the differences between what they attribute to each other and what is true.

Observer

The non–judgmental function that notices you in the moment— both your internal states and behavior. It is your observer that enables you to choose what to do while in an interaction.

Patterns

A habitual, repetitive sequence of events that, when begun, lead to highly predictable outcomes. When applied to interactions, patterns can be viewed metaphorically as a dance; a sequence of habitual steps that lead to predictable results.

Self

A unified totality of all the processes and structures that define an individual.

Thoughts

These are the cognitive meanings you ascribe to both internal and external stimuli.

Triangulation

A triangle is formed by any three persons or issues. Triangulation happens when any two parts of a system become uncomfortable with one another and therefore focus upon a third person or issue as a way of stabilizing their relationship.

Undifferentiated Interactions

In an undifferentiated interaction neither party has direct descriptive, here–and–now information about each other's thoughts, feelings and wants. Individuals in the interactions react from their internal stories about each other, not from direct, shared, descriptive information.

Wants

These are the desires and intentions that you have for yourself, the other, and your here–and–now interaction.

About the Author

Ron Short is currently owner of Learning In Action Technologies, a consulting, training and publishing firm dedicated to helping people learn from each other. Ron's years as an educator, director of an innovative graduate program, consultant and most recently as President of The Leadership Group, have confirmed three fundamental beliefs.

1. Mistrust is often the epicenter of organizational chaos, pain and waste.

2. These costs can be transformed into profitable, productive energy when people learn to trust each other and themselves.

3. This transformation does not come about by magic. It requires vigilance, self–awareness and the disciplined application of values, principles, and skills—all of which contribute to collective learning.

Ron's professional purpose is to help people make and sustain that transformation.

Ron received his doctorate in psychology from Claremont Graduate School in 1965; was an intern with the National Training Laboratories in 1969; co-created a Master of Arts program in the Applied Behavioral Sciences; and with John Runyan, founded The Leadership Group. He has consulted and trained extensively in the United States and abroad and has written numerous articles in professional journals. He has written two prior books; *A Special Kind Of Leadership: The Key to Learning Organizations* and *Learning from Your Experience With People.*